BRAIN GAMES

Sherlock Holmes
Puzzles

Gather the clues and solve the case!

Publications International, Ltd.

Let's get social!

@Publications_International

@PublicationsInternational

@BrainGames.TM

www.pilbooks.com

It's Elementary

For a character first introduced in print in 1887, Sherlock Holmes is still going strong. Generations of readers and mystery aficionados have enjoyed the adventures of the sleuth and his sidekick, Dr. Watson, as well as numerous stage and screen adaptations. Those adventures were the inspiration for this book, *Sherlock Holmes Puzzles*. Do you have Sherlock Holmes' keen eyes and attention to detail? You can prove it by solving mystery-themed visual puzzles. Do you have his logical abilities? The book offers logic puzzles, word searches, cryptograms, and more. Along the way, you'll also get to test your knowledge of the Doyle canon with plenty of Holmes trivia.

Don't worry if you find yourself getting stuck occasionally—even Watson needed a bit of explanation from time to time! Answers are located at the back of the book when you need a helpful boost. So grab your pencil—and a deerstalker cap, if you'd like—and get ready to detect.

A "Smell Oh Shocker" Anagram

Below is a quotation from a Sherlock Holmes story. Fill in the blanks in each sentence with a word that is an anagram (rearrangement) of the capitalized word(s). Bonus: Name the Sherlock Holmes adventure from which this quotation is drawn.

I had neither kith nor kin in England, and was therefore as free as Air— or as free as an COIN ME _income_ of eleven shillings and sixpence a day will TRIP ME _permit_ a man to be. Under such circumstances, I naturally gravitated to London, that great COP SOLES _____ into which all the LOSER GNU _____ and idlers of the Empire are irresistibly drained. There I stayed for some time at a RAVE TIP _____ hotel in the Strand, leading a FORCES MOLTS _____, meaningless existence, and spending such money as I had, considerably more EEL FRY _____ than I ought. So MARGINAL _____ did the state of my SCAN FINE _____ become, that I soon realized that I must either leave the metropolis and CRATE SUIT _____ somewhere in the country, or that I must make a complete ALIEN TAROT _____ in my style of living. Choosing the latter alternative, I began by making up my mind to leave the hotel, and to take up my quarters in some less ENTRIES POUT _____ and less expensive ICED LIMO _____.

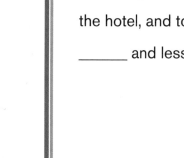

imprct
mipert
pimert

What Do You See? (Part I)

Study this picture of the crime scene for 1 minute, then turn the page.

What Do You See? (Part II)

(Do not read this until you have read the previous page!) Which image exactly matches the crime scene?

1

2

3

4

A "Sol Ohm Hecklers" Anagram

Below is a quotation from a Sherlock Holmes story. Fill in the blanks in each sentence with a word that is an anagram (rearrangement) of the capitalized word(s). Bonus: Name the Sherlock Holmes adventure from which this quotation is drawn.

"Really, Watson, you excel SOLE FURY _____," said Holmes, pushing back his chair and lighting a cigarette. "I am bound to say that in all the NO CACTUS _____ which you have been so good as to give of my own small CAVEMEN HEIST _____ you have habitually RUNE TRADED _____ your own abilities. It may be that you are not yourself US UM LION _____, but you are a conductor of light. Some people without SIS SPONGES _____ genius have a remarkable power of SAILING MUTT _____ it. I confess, my dear ELF OWL _____, that I am very much in your debt."

Answers on page 346.

Famous First Lines

How well do you know the Holmes canon? Match the first line of each story to the story's title.

1. Mr. Sherlock Holmes, who was usually very late in the mornings, save upon those not infrequent occasions when he was up all night, was seated at the breakfast table.

2. In the year 1878 I took my degree of Doctor of Medicine of the University of London, and proceeded to Netley to go through the course prescribed for surgeons in the army.

3. Sherlock Holmes took his bottle from the corner of the mantel-piece and his hypodermic syringe from its neat morocco case.

4. To Sherlock Holmes she is always THE woman.

5. I had called upon my friend, Mr. Sherlock Holmes, one day in the autumn of last year and found him in deep conversation with a very stout, florid-faced, elderly gentleman with fiery red hair.

A. The Sign of the Four

B. A Scandal in Bohemia

C. The Hound of the Baskervilles

D. A Study in Scarlet

E. The Red-Headed League

Answers on page 346.

What Changed? (Part I)

The consulting detective was at a house party. What did he see in the toolshed? Examine the objects, then turn the page.

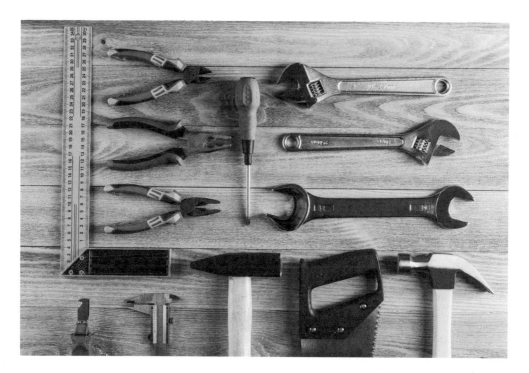

What Changed? (Part II)

There was a murder at the house party! The consulting detective immediately spotted that one object changed position, and that object was found to be the hastily cleaned murder weapon. From memory, can you work out what changed position?

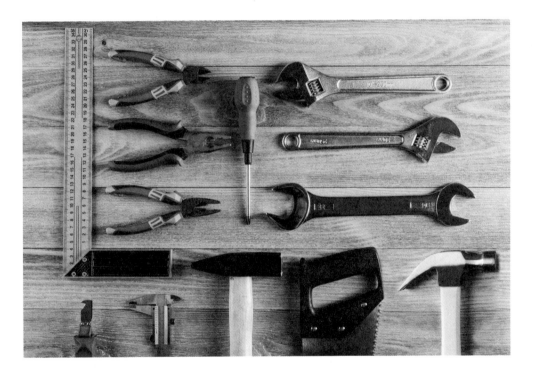

What Went Missing? (Part I)

The consulting detective met her client on Wednesday, and was told that some old family documents were hidden somewhere in the room. This was the room in which they met. Examine the room, then turn the page.

What Went Missing? (Part II)

On Friday, the consulting detective was called back because her client had disappeared. The consulting detective noted that something else had gone missing. From memory, can you work out what went missing?

Tracking the Hound of the Baskervilles

Fill in the blank! Complete each quote from "The Hound of the Baskervilles" with one of the choices.

1. "A cast of your _____, sir, until the original is available, would be an ornament to any anthropological museum."

   A. teeth   **B.** skull   **C.** fingers

2. "The detection of _____ is one of the most elementary branches of knowledge to the special expert in crime, though I confess that once when I was very young I confused the "Leeds Mercury" with the "Western Morning News.""

   A. types   **B.** footprints   **C.** newspaper clippings

3. "There is nothing more _____ than a case where everything goes against you."

   A. aggravating   **B.** stimulating   **C.** wonderful

4. "The world is full of _____ things which nobody by any chance ever observes."

   A. elementary   **B.** mysterious   **C.** obvious

5. "The past and the present are within the field of my _____, but what a man may do in the future is a hard question to answer."

   A. deductions   **B.** inquiry   **C.** observations

Answers on page 347.

The Hound of the Baskervilles

Each word or phrase in all capitals in the Sherlock Holmes quotation below is contained within the group of letters. Words can be found horizontally, vertically, or diagonally. They may read either forward or backward.

"I find that before the TERRIBLE event occurred several people had seen a CREATURE upon the MOOR which corresponds with this BASKERVILLE demon, and which could not possibly be any ANIMAL known to SCIENCE. They all agreed that it was a huge creature, LUMINOUS, GHASTLY, and SPECTRAL. I have CROSS-EXAMINED these men, one of them a HARD-HEADED countryman, one a FARRIER, and one a moorland FARMER, who all tell the same story of this dreadful APPARITION, exactly corresponding to the HELL-HOUND of the LEGEND. I assure you that there is a REIGN OF TERROR in the district, and that it is a hardy man who will cross the moor at night."

```
P D A D Q O D C C O W C Q G P
X E P E C L R F V H G D H R O
J D P N J D U A K C G A E O Y
U A A I A W F L A U S I S G Y
T E R M N J A R B T G Q B L S
E H I A I D S Z L N Z A A U E
L D T X M N Y Y O X S R O C F
B R I E A E P F Q K T N N E A
I A O S L G T A E C I E V N R
R H N S N E E R E M I H S L R
R Y J O R L V P U C M S U X I
E E T R T I S L S M K E Q L E
T Q O C L H A H O F A R M E R
C R O L D N U O H L L E H U P
C R E A T U R E G I T G H X S
```

Answers on page 347.

A Sad Statistic

Cryptograms are messages in substitution code. Break the code to read the message. For example, THE SMART CAT might become FVO QWGDF JGF if **F** is substituted for **T, V** for **H, O** for **E,** and so on.

RDA MAOZAJRKCA LB QRLHAJ KOR

RDKR EQ OAZLTAOAP EQ JLR TAOX

DECD. LJHX BETA RL RAJ MAOZAJR

IECDR WA OAZLTAOAP.

What Went Missing? (Part I)

The consulting detective met his client on Monday, and was told that some old family documents were hidden somewhere in the room. This was the room in which they met. Examine the room, then turn the page.

What Went Missing? (Part II)

On Tuesday, the consulting detective was called back because his client had disappeared. The consulting detective noted that something else had gone missing. From memory, can you work out what went missing?

What Went Missing? (Part I)

The consulting detective was at a house party. What did she see in the garden shed? Examine the objects, then turn the page.

What Went Missing? (Part II)

There was a murder at the house party! The consulting detective immediately spotted that one object went missing, and that object was probably the murder weapon. From memory, can you work out what went missing?

A Study in Sherlock

Fill in the blank! Complete each quote from "A Study in Scarlet" with one of the choices.

1. "How are you?" he said cordially, gripping my hand with a strength for which I should hardly have given him credit. "You have been in _____, I perceive."

   A. Afghanistan   **B.** Devonshire   **C.** hospital

2. His _____ was as remarkable as his knowledge.

   A. range of interests   **B.** curiosity   **C.** ignorance

3. There was one little sallow rat-faced, dark-eyed fellow who was introduced to me as _____, and who came three or four times in a single week.

   A. Inspector Gregson   **B.** Mr. Lestrade   **C.** Inspector Lestrade

4. "By a man's finger nails, by his coat-sleeve, by his boot, by his trouser knees, by the callosities of his forefinger and thumb, by his expression, by his shirt cuffs—by each of these things a man's _____ is plainly revealed."

   A. calling   **B.** address   **C.** location

5. "No doubt you think that you are complimenting me in comparing me to _____," he observed. "Now, in my opinion, _____ was a very inferior fellow.

   A. Lecoq   **B.** Bertillon   **C.** Dupin

Answers on page 347.

The Hound of the Baskervilles Characters

Every word listed is contained within the group of letters. Words can be found in a straight line horizontally, vertically, or diagonally. They may be read either forward or backward.

CHARLES	JOHN
CONVICT	LAURA LYONS
ELIZA	MISS STAPLETON
FRANKLAND	MORTIMER
HENRY	SHERLOCK HOLMES
HUGO	WATSON
JACK	

```
S P E D K N S R E M I T R O M
E K J C W B V E O T W T S Y N
M B A F R A N K L A N D H O C
L J R C T B J T H R A E T K V
O K L P H U K M R I A E M T U
H S K P S Y Y N R Q L H Y L Q
K X N V U T I K J P O H C U H
C P I O P Y Q E A H H E N R Y
O N K I Y A I T D T Z G S W C
L X G O P L S S J H S S T T J
R E G P P S A U Q H H P H R P
E U L G S S R R C O N V I C T
H E H I X R W A U W A T S O N
S K M Y Z V X S J A V G B Y N
N H O J E A C R A L L U R A C
```

Answers on page 347.

The Curse of the Baskervilles Pt. 1

Each word or phrase in all capitals in the Sherlock Holmes quotation below is contained within the group of letters. Words can be found horizontally, vertically, or diagonally. They may read either forward or backward.

"Of the ORIGIN of the Hound of the BASKERVILLES there have been many STATEMENTS, yet as I come in a DIRECT line from Hugo Baskerville, and as I had the STORY from my FATHER, who also had it from his, I have set it down with all BELIEF that it OCCURRED even as is here set forth. And I would have you believe, my sons, that the same JUSTICE which PUNISHES sin may also most GRACIOUSLY forgive it, and that no ban is so heavy but that by PRAYER and REPENTANCE it may be removed. Learn then from this story not to fear the FRUITS of the past, but rather to be CIRCUMSPECT in the FUTURE, that those foul PASSIONS whereby our family has SUFFERED so GRIEVOUSLY may not again be loosed to our UNDOING.

```
Y Z Y X N R P R A Y E R F D W
L B H Q C B K R L W J W R E X
S Y A V M J E Q E I Q P U R Y
U L N S W D S L T H Z M I E C
O S A I K Z E G I A T O T F I
V U C S Y E B R N E R A S F R
E O F U T U R E R I F N F U C
I I I K D A R V G U O P E S U
R C M X I C T I I I C D Y X M
G A U F R M N E S L G C N D S
C R S J E A P S M W L J O U P
J G T E C N A T N E P E R Q E
J Y O N T P W Z A X N J S H C
D S R J U S T I C E Z T O E T
C B Y P U N I S H E S V S A X
```

Answers on page 347.

Each word or phrase in all capitals in the Sherlock Holmes quotation below is contained within the group of letters. Words can be found horizontally, vertically, or diagonally. They may read either forward or backward.

"Know then that in the time of the GREAT REBELLION (the history of which by the learned LORD CLARENDON I most EARNESTLY commend to your ATTENTION) this MANOR of Baskerville was held by Hugo of that name, nor can it be GAINSAID that he was a most wild, PROFANE, and GODLESS man. This, in truth, his neighbours might have PARDONED, seeing that saints have never FLOURISHED in those parts, but there was in him a certain WANTON and CRUEL humour which made his name a BYWORD through the WEST. It chanced that this Hugo came to LOVE (if, indeed, so dark a passion may be known under so BRIGHT a name) the daughter of a YEOMAN who held lands near the Baskerville estate. But the young MAIDEN, being DISCREET and of good REPUTE, would ever avoid him, for she feared his EVIL NAME.

```
T D Z M I X C R T H V B Y L L
N T E D I S C R E E T V H O O
T R W H R R Z Y U D Y F V B R
S D I A S N I A G E I E W Y D
P I J J E I K H O X L A D W C
G R O N A M R M B H N G E O L
T H G I R B A U B T O W N R A
P A I D E N R N O D L S O D R
R R S N P P M N L L K T D O E
O I R E U V H E H I F D R T N
F W B D T S S C H G V W A L D
A E I I E S K Y T B Q E P Y O
N S M A N O I T N E T T A N N
E T J M E A R N E S T L Y M F
G R E A T R E B E L L I O N F
```

Answers on page 348.

The Curse of the Baskervilles Pt. 3

Each word or phrase in all capitals in the Sherlock Holmes quotation below is contained within the group of letters. Words can be found horizontally, vertically, or diagonally. They may read either forward or backward.

So it came to pass that one MICHAELMAS this Hugo, with five or six of his idle and WICKED COMPANIONS, stole down upon the FARM and carried off the maiden, her FATHER and BROTHERS being from home, as he well knew. When they had brought her to the Hall the maiden was placed in an UPPER CHAMBER, while Hugo and his friends sat down to a long CAROUSE, as was their nightly CUSTOM. Now, the poor LASS upstairs was like to have her WITS turned at the SINGING AND SHOUTING and terrible OATHS which came up to her from below, for they say that the words used by Hugo Baskerville, when he was in WINE, were such as might blast the man who said them. At last in the STRESS of her fear she did that which might have DAUNTED the bravest or most active man, for by the aid of the growth of IVY which covered (and still covers) the south wall she came down from under the eaves, and so HOMEWARD across the MOOR, there being three leagues BETWIXT the Hall and her father's farm.

```
F O A I F A T H E R C D L H H I U U J
B S L A X Z I H A Y M A U A R V D U L
H E T T E A R Z N I V A R U S R N T B
K O T R S T I W C V J D P O E S Y Q Q
T Q M B E T B H U V H D U B U I H Z E
X X J E X S A R Z R K G M M I S A Y G
M L I S W E S I R Q D A I A O W E P F
X C N W L A M E F L H J W V M O Q L Z
Y G C M T Q R O A C M L D B X C R J Z
B K A H M E A D R Z L U G F X P L L V
T S A C Q T B E M X G X P L E F M G L
R O C U H L P D K R B V D E T N U A D
S M O S C P J U Z H P R E E R Y G A O
G N I T U O H S D N A G N I G N I S G
B O Y O N S R E H T O R B L E R F C T
L M T M S R T A R B P Q R S Y K L S E
W I C K E D C O M P A N I O N S C V R
E N I W Y O B M F J Y D L T Z D T D B
M J Z D O I S C D E P K D I V Y L F C
```

Answers on page 348.

The Curse of the Baskervilles Pt. 4

Each word or phrase in all capitals in the Sherlock Holmes quotation below is contained within the group of letters. Words can be found horizontally, vertically, or diagonally. They may read either forward or backward.

"It chanced that some LITTLE time later Hugo left his guests to carry FOOD AND DRINK—with other worse things, PERCHANCE—to his CAPTIVE, and so found the CAGE empty and the bird ESCAPED. Then, as it would seem, he became as one that hath a DEVIL, for, rushing down the stairs into the dining-hall, he sprang upon the great table, FLAGONS and TRENCHERS flying before him, and he cried aloud before all the company that he would that very night render his body and soul to the POWERS OF EVIL if he might but overtake the WENCH. And while the REVELLERS stood AGHAST at the fury of the man, one more wicked or, it may be, more DRUNKEN than the rest, cried out that they should put the hounds upon her. Whereat Hugo ran from the house, crying to his GROOMS that they should SADDLE his mare and UNKENNEL the pack, and giving the hounds a KERCHIEF of the maid's, he swung them to the line, and so off full cry in the MOONLIGHT over the moor.

```
L X E H A A X F E F L S E P A
I D S A D D L E E R E R T E N
V A V D U A C I M R N E H R E
E L T L G A H Z O K N L G C K
F Q I O P C R Y W R E L I H N
O P N T R H D J S M K E L A U
S S I E T U P E T F N V N N R
R V K F G L P R S S U E O C D
E Z Z I R X E X J C A R O E D
W Z W F I N O O A D A H M O K
O W E N C H W G J E F P G Q C
P P T H I N E Q N V W A E A T
H M E A Q E N K I I U K W D U
O R U S M O O R G L O R U I Q
S F O O D A N D D R I N K P W
```

Answers on page 348.

Each word or phrase in all capitals in the Sherlock Holmes quotation below is contained within the group of letters. Words can be found horizontally, vertically, or diagonally. They may read either forward or backward.

"Now, for some space the revellers stood AGAPE, unable to understand all that had been done in such HASTE. But anon their BEMUSED WITS awoke to the NATURE of the DEED which was like to be done upon the MOORLANDS. Everything was now in an UPROAR, some calling for their PISTOLS, some for their HORSES, and some for another FLASK of wine. But at length some sense came back to their CRAZED MINDS, and the whole of them, THIRTEEN in number, took horse and started in PURSUIT. The moon shone CLEAR above them, and they rode SWIFTLY abreast, taking that COURSE which the maid must needs have taken if she were to reach her own home.

```
H P S N A T U R E H O T B W E
O Z B M P U R S U I T U Y S P
R C R A Z E D M I N D S R B A
S S S A E K Q A D N Y U K F G
E B D X S X F Y P W O K S A A
S Q L N W T L Z V C W J A O Z
K P H K A T G R M B R E L J K
G P K Z F L I D I D U D F R M
E E F I B E R D R N D A E K C
F T W J B K S O L J L S G E Y
B S Y E W I S L O T S I P F D
Z X S N T L X S Q M N M D M U
Z B E M U S E D W I T S T I V
R S O Z Q F A T H I R T E E N
R A O R P U J H R A E L C G S
```

Answers on page 348.

Each word or phrase in all capitals in the Sherlock Holmes quotation below is contained within the group of letters. Words can be found horizontally, vertically, or diagonally. They may read either forward or backward.

They had gone a MILE or two when they passed one of the NIGHT SHEPHERDS upon the moorlands, and they CRIED to him to know if he had seen the HUNT. And the man, as the story goes, was so CRAZED with FEAR that he could SCARCE speak, but at last he said that he had INDEED seen the UNHAPPY maiden, with the hounds upon her track. 'But I have seen more than that,' said he, 'for Hugo Baskerville passed me upon his BLACK MARE, and there ran MUTE behind him such a HOUND OF HELL as God FORBID should ever be at my HEELS.' So the drunken SQUIRES cursed the shepherd and rode ONWARD.

```
K  N  Y  P  P  A  H  N  U  D  G  N  G  R  D
C  S  G  H  L  R  K  P  G  F  H  G  T  I  R
I  O  D  H  E  I  N  D  E  E  D  I  B  V  E
H  D  O  R  N  E  R  T  E  I  H  R  F  I  C
Z  U  I  Z  E  V  L  R  N  O  O  Z  O  F  R
Q  P  N  N  B  H  A  S  U  F  O  G  L  F  A
M  W  J  T  M  M  P  N  M  X  X  Q  W  S  C
K  N  I  U  K  H  D  E  Z  M  D  I  Q  H  S
D  X  T  C  W  O  W  I  H  W  G  U  B  C  J
G  E  A  O  F  E  D  G  G  S  I  N  P  R  Q
X  L  Z  H  N  F  E  A  R  R  T  A  V  I  B
B  A  E  A  N  W  K  T  E  N  O  H  X  E  H
P  L  L  L  R  Y  A  S  V  F  O  Y  G  D  U
L  Q  K  I  I  C  I  R  X  A  V  O  A  I  X
T  G  U  Y  A  M  G  E  D  N  G  Q  R  S  N
```

Answers on page 349.

The Curse of the Baskervilles Pt. 7

Each word or phrase in all capitals in the Sherlock Holmes quotation below is contained within the group of letters. Words can be found horizontally, vertically, or diagonally. They may read either forward or backward.

But soon their SKINS turned COLD, for there came a GALLOPING across the moor, and the black mare, DABBLED with WHITE FROTH, went past with TRAILING bridle and EMPTY SADDLE. Then the revellers rode close together, for a great fear was on them, but they still FOLLOWED over the moor, though each, had he been ALONE, would have been right GLAD to have turned his horse's head. Riding SLOWLY in this FASHION they came at last upon the hounds. These, though known for their VALOUR and their breed, were WHIMPERING in a CLUSTER at the head of a DEEP DIP or GOYAL, as we call it, upon the moor, some slinking away and some, with starting HACKLES and STARING EYES, gazing down the narrow VALLEY before them.

```
K E O P S W H I M P E R I N G
E N O L A L L E L C S K I N S
F G U Q B C O A L Z E N V A D
O Q N X N Y X W Y Y M D A C R
L N O I H S A F L O T E L L E
L Q V N P G L A D Y G E L U R
O D L O C O H O F J B P E S W
W T Q Q V A L U M B G D Y T T
E B J D C V A L O U R I B E D
D C P K S B N L A B P P Y R E
F M L S T A R I N G E Y E S L
N E M P T Y S A D D L E A J B
S O H T O R F E T I H W M X B
H S Z W G C N I M N B T V B A
F J O T R A I L I N G A L L D
```

Answers on page 349.

The Curse of the Baskervilles Pt. 8

Each word or phrase in all capitals in the Sherlock Holmes quotation below is contained within the group of letters. Words can be found horizontally, vertically, or diagonally. They may read either forward or backward.

The COMPANY had come to a HALT, more SOBER men, as you may GUESS, than when they started. The most of them would by no means ADVANCE, but three of them, the BOLDEST, or it may be the most DRUNKEN, rode FORWARD down the goyal. Now, it opened into a BROAD SPACE in which stood two of those great STONES, still to be seen there, which were set by certain FORGOTTEN peoples in the DAYS OF OLD. The MOON was SHINING bright upon the CLEARING, and there in the CENTRE lay the UNHAPPY maid where she had fallen, DEAD of fear and of FATIGUE.

```
M S H I N I N G O N E N D
O S C D H W U S E T Z E A
O Y E P D J M U S S L T Y
N P G N L A G M H E G T S
V P R T O I E H X D U O O
H A L T T T F D A L V G F
T H T A K E S I I O L R O
G N F O R W A R D B D O L
S U W T Y N A P M O C F D
V O N N J L A D V A N C E
Q E B R O A D S P A C E W
C C L E A R I N G T K T J
Y X V D R U N K E N U C D
```

The Curse of the Baskervilles Pt. 9

Each word or phrase in all capitals in the Sherlock Holmes quotation below is contained within the group of letters. Words can be found horizontally, vertically, or diagonally. They may read either forward or backward.

But it was not the sight of her BODY, nor yet was it that of the body of Hugo Baskerville lying near her, which RAISED the hair upon the heads of these three DAREDEVIL roysterers, but it was that, standing over Hugo, and PLUCKING at his THROAT, there stood a FOUL thing, a great, BLACK BEAST, shaped like a HOUND, yet larger than any hound that ever MORTAL eye has rested upon. And even as they looked the thing tore the throat out of Hugo Baskerville, on which, as it turned its BLAZING eyes and DRIPPING jaws upon them, the three SHRIEKED with fear and rode for DEAR LIFE, still SCREAMING, across the moor. One, it is said, died that very night of what he had seen, and the other TWAIN were but BROKEN MEN for the rest of their days.

```
G B L A C K B E A S T N E
N R A I S E D L N Y K E I
I G H L F I D F U D Z M X
P N S A R Z O N A O L N D
P I C T O Q B R U D F E F
I K R R L G E K Q O A K P
R C E O Y D O B N R H O F
D U A M E S S I L U L R T
L L M V Y Z A I D Y I B T
B P I J P W F T H R O A T
H L N C T E L P L V R T H
W N G V I S H R I E K E D
T B L A Z I N G K A P U D
```

Answers on page 349.

The Curse of the Baskervilles Pt. 10

Each word or phrase in all capitals in the Sherlock Holmes quotation below is contained within the group of letters. Words can be found horizontally, vertically, or diagonally. They may read either forward or backward.

Such is the TALE, my SONS, of the coming of the hound which is said to have PLAGUED the family so SORELY ever since. If I have set it down it is because that which is clearly known hath less TERROR than that which is but HINTED at and GUESSED. Nor can it be DENIED that many of the FAMILY have been unhappy in their deaths, which have been sudden, BLOODY, and MYSTERIOUS. Yet may we SHELTER ourselves in the INFINITE goodness of PROVIDENCE, which would not FOREVER punish the innocent beyond that third or fourth GENERATION which is threatened in holy writ. To that Providence, my sons, I hereby COMMEND you, and I COUNSEL you by way of CAUTION to forbear from crossing the moor in those DARK HOURS when the powers of evil are EXALTED.

```
S B S U O I R E T S Y M D C G
H O Y P D N W T B L A A A O U
E P N D S E B V E Q G U R M E
L L R M O I R R C E X C K M S
T A E W S O O Y N F P A H E S
E G V S T S L E E C D U O N E
R U E G N I R B C T M T U D D
S E R S M A D P N O U I R C I
K D O A T G E Z E H U O S R F
I N F I N I T E D O J N E Y D
Y F O E I E L A I S N O S E F
F N T C R S A S V I L J I E L
M K K R Z O X T O H W N K S L
H V O U H M E F R P E G G U Q
J R H I N T E D P D E L A T F
```

Answers on page 350.

A "Her Loss Hemlock" Anagram

Below is a quotation from a Sherlock Holmes story. Fill in the blanks in each sentence with a word that is an anagram (rearrangement) of the capitalized word(s). Bonus: Name the Sherlock Holmes adventure from which this quotation is drawn.

"It is SPICY LIMIT _____ itself," he remarked, chuckling at my surprise,–"so DAY BLURS _____ simple that an explanation is RUEFUL SOUPS _____; and yet it may serve to define the limits of BONSAI TROVE _____ and of DICE DONUT _____. VIBRATE SOON _____ tells me that you have a little reddish mould HI DANGER _____ to your instep. Just PIPE SOOT _____ the Seymour Street Office they have taken up the NAVE TEMP _____ and thrown up some earth which lies in such a way that it is difficult to avoid GRADIENT _____ in it in entering. The earth is of this peculiar HERS DID _____ tint which is found, as far as I know, WHEREON _____ else in the neighborhood. So much is BOA INVESTOR _____. The rest is COD UNTIED _____."

"How, then, did you deduce the RAGE MELT _____?"

"Why, of course I knew that you had not RENT WIT _____ a letter, since I sat opposite to you all GIN NORM _____. I see also in your open desk there that you have a sheet of stamps and a thick bundle of post-cards. What could you go into the post-office for, then, but to send a wire? MAIN ELITE _____ all other FAR COTS _____, and the one which MARINES _____ must be the truth."

What Went Missing? (Part I)

The consulting detective met her client in the library about some thefts. Examine the room she saw, then turn the page.

What Went Missing? (Part II)

The following day, the client called the consulting detective back about more thefts. The client challenged the consulting detective to spot what had been stolen. From memory, can you work out what went missing?

A "Ms Holler Chokes" Anagram

Below is a quotation from a Sherlock Holmes story. Fill in the blanks in each sentence with a word that is an anagram (rearrangement) of the capitalized word(s). Bonus: Name the Sherlock Holmes adventure from which this quotation is drawn.

"Porlock, Watson, is a POMMEL DUNE _____, a mere identification mark; but behind it lies a shifty and VISA EVE _____ personality. In a former letter he RANK FLY _____ informed me that the name was not his own, and FEE DID _____ me ever to trace him among the MEET-ING _____ millions of this great city. Porlock is important, not for HE FILMS _____, but for the great man with whom he is in touch. PUT RICE _____ to yourself the pilot fish with the HARKS _____, the jackal with the lion—anything that is insignificant in companionship with what is BAILED FROM _____: not only FEDORA LIMB _____, Watson, but ITS SIREN _____—in the highest degree SIRE SNIT _____. That is where he comes within my purview. You have heard me speak of FOR SPORES _____ ARMY TRIO _____?"

 Answers on page 350.

Interception

You've intercepted a message that is meant to reveal a location for an upcoming meeting between two criminal masterminds. The only problem is, the message shows many place names. Can you figure out the right location?

CROATIA

FINLAND

CHILE

GRENADA

GHANA

SAMOA

Crack the Password

A detective has found a memory aid that the criminal left behind, a list of coded passwords. The detective knows that the criminal likes to scramble each password, then remove the same letter from each word. Can you figure out the missing letter and unscramble each word in this set to reveal the passwords?

MENTOR

PIANOS

REPEAL

CRUELLY

Answers on page 351.

For Stage and Screen

Every name below belongs to an actor who played the role of Watson in a Sherlock Holmes adaptation. Names can be found in a straight line horizontally, vertically, or diagonally. They may be read either forward or backward.

ALAN COX	HUBERT WILLIS
BEN KINGSLEY	JUDE LAW
BRUCE MCRAE	MARTIN FREEMAN
COLIN BLAKELY	NIGEL BRUCE
DAVID BURKE	PATRICK MACNEE
DONALD PICKERING	RAYMOND FRANCIS
EDWARD HARDWICKE	ROBERT DUVALL
H. KYRLE BELLEW	ROLAND YOUNG

```
D O N A L D P I C K E R I N G
A K K B N B R U C E M C R A E
V R A Y M O N D F R A N C I S
I Q Y X O C N A L A Q Q Y R R
D G N U O Y D N A L O R W O F
B E N K I N G S L E Y H F B B
U I N I G E L B R U C E X E V
R T R H T F Q S C D Q J S R M
K W P O J X D Y R Y U V I T H
E K C I W D R A H D R A W D E
M A R T I N F R E E M A N U I
W E L L E B E L R Y K H C V T
H X E E N C A M K C I R T A P
S I L L I W T R E B U H M L V
W J M C O L I N B L A K E L Y
```

Answers on page 351.

Interception

You've intercepted a message that is meant to reveal a location for an upcoming meeting between two criminal masterminds. The only problem is, the message shows many place names. Can you figure out the right location?

ICELAND

LESOTHO

TONGA

INDIA

COMOROS

BENIN

A "Shh Mole Locker" Anagram

Below is a quotation from a Sherlock Holmes story. Fill in the blanks in each sentence with a word that is an anagram (rearrangement) of the capitalized word(s). Bonus: Name the Sherlock Holmes adventure from which this quotation is drawn.

"You will remember that I remarked the other day, just before we went into the very IMPELS _____ problem presented by Miss Mary Sutherland, that for strange effects and ERRATA RID ONYX _____ combinations we must go to life itself, which is always far more AD RING _____ than any effort of the I GO MAINTAIN _____."

"A proposition which I took the BILE TRY _____ of BIND GOUT _____."

"You did, COT ROD _____, but none the less you must come round to my view, for otherwise I shall keep on GIN LIP _____ fact upon fact on you until your reason breaks down under them and WACKO LEGENDS _____ me to be right. Now, Mr. Jabez Wilson here has been good enough to call upon me this morning, and to begin a RA-VINE RAT _____ which promises to be one of the most SLAG RUIN _____ which I have listened to for some time. You have heard me re-mark that the ANGST REST _____ and most unique things are very often DECENT CON _____ not with the larger but with the smaller MRS ICE _____, and occasionally, indeed, where there is room for doubt whether any TOP IVIES _____ crime has been committed. As far as I have heard it is MOBILE SIPS _____ for me to say whether the present case is an ANCIENTS _____ of crime or not, but the course of events is CLEAR TINY _____ among the most SNUG LIAR _____ that I have ever listened to."

   Answers on page 351.

A Study in Sherlock

Early in his acquaintance with Sherlock Holmes, Dr. Watson wrote: "I pondered over our short conversation, however, and endeavoured to draw my deductions from it. He said that he would acquire no knowledge which did not bear upon his object. Therefore all the knowledge which he possessed was such as would be useful to him. I enumerated in my own mind all the various points upon which he had shown me that he was exceptionally well-informed. I even took a pencil and jotted them down. I could not help smiling at the document when I had completed it."

Can you match each category with Watson's descriptions of Holmes' knowledge in that category? Some descriptions are used for more than one category.

Accurate, but unsystematic   Practical, but limited

Feeble   Profound

Immense   Variable

Nil

1. Literature _____

2. Philosophy _____

3. Astronomy _____

4. Politics _____

5. Botany _____

6. Geology _____

7. Chemistry _____

8. Anatomy _____

9. Sensational Literature _____

Crack the Password

A detective has found a memory aid that the criminal left behind, a list of coded passwords. The detective knows that the criminal likes to scramble each password, then remove the same letter from each word. Can you figure out the missing letter and unscramble each word in this set to reveal the passwords?

PARCEL

RESEATED

PILFER

UNIT

Answers on page 352.

Famous First Lines

How well do you know the Holmes canon? Match the first line of each story to the story's title.

1. When I glance over my notes and records of the Sherlock Holmes cases between the years '82 and '90, I am faced by so many which present strange and interesting features that it is no easy matter to know which to choose and which to leave.

2. Mrs. Hudson, the landlady of Sherlock Holmes, was a long-suffering woman.

3. It was no very unusual thing for Mr. Lestrade, of Scotland Yard, to look in upon us of an evening, and his visits were welcome to Sherlock Holmes, for they enabled him to keep in touch with all that was going on at the police headquarters.

4. "I am afraid, Watson, that I shall have to go," said Holmes, as we sat down together to our breakfast one morning.

5. "I have some papers here," said my friend Sherlock Holmes, as we sat one winter's night on either side of the fire, "which I really think, Watson, that it would be worth your while to glance over."

A. The Adventure of Silver Blaze

B. The Five Orange Pips

C. The Adventure of the "Gloria Scott"

D. The Adventure of the Dying Detective

E. The Adventure of the Six Napoleons

Answers on page 352.

A "Chrome Elk Slosh" Anagram

Below is a quotation from a Sherlock Holmes story. Fill in the blanks in each sentence with a word that is an anagram (rearrangement) of the capitalized word(s). Bonus: Name the Sherlock Holmes adventure from which this quotation is drawn.

To Sherlock Holmes she is always THE woman. I have seldom heard him OMEN TIN _____ her under any other name. In his eyes she EELS PICS _____ and predominates the whole of her sex. It was not that he felt any MIEN TOO _____ akin to love for Irene Adler. All MOTE IONS _____, and that one particularly, were BARREN HOT _____ to his cold, precise but admirably CABAL DEN _____ mind. He was, I take it, the most perfect reasoning and observing AH MINCE _____ that the world has seen, but as a lover he would have placed himself in a false POTION IS _____. He never spoke of the softer SOAP SINS _____, save with a gibe and a sneer. They were DRAMA BILE _____ things for the observer—excellent for drawing the veil from men's TOE VIMS _____ and actions. But for the trained reasoner to admit such UNION STIRS _____ into his own delicate and finely adjusted MANE TEMPTER _____was to introduce a distracting factor which might throw a doubt upon all his mental results. Grit in a sensitive NUTRIMENTS _____, or a crack in one of his own high-power lenses, would not be more BUSING DIRT _____ than a strong emotion in a nature such as his. And yet there was but one woman to him, and that woman was the late Irene Adler, of dubious and ELOQUENT BIAS _____ memory.

 Answers on page 352.

A Mysterious Event

Cryptograms are messages in substitution code. Break the code to read the message. For example, THE SMART CAT might become FVO QWGDF JGF if **F** is substituted for **T**, **V** for **H**, **O** for **E**, and so on.

SCI YITO 1911 DKVLGVIJ T KLSTPGI

RTQI LA TOS SCIAS–SCI HLKT GDQT

WTQ QSLGIK AOLH SCI GLUVOI PY TK

IHMGLYII. CI WTQ RTUBCS SWL YITOQ

GTSIO TKJ SCI MTDKSDKB WTQ

OISUOKIJ SL DSQ CLHI.

Interception

You've intercepted a message that is meant to reveal a location for an upcoming meeting between two criminal masterminds. The only problem is, the message shows many place names. Can you figure out the right location?

WASHINGTON D.C.

PHNOM PENH

HELSINKI

FOND DU LAC

ATLANTA

PHILIPSBURG

OSLO

A "Clerks Shoo Helm" Anagram

Below is a quotation from a Sherlock Holmes story. Fill in the blanks in each sentence with a word that is an anagram (rearrangement) of the capitalized word(s). Bonus: Name the Sherlock Holmes adventure from which this quotation is drawn.

"My dear fellow," said Sherlock Holmes as we sat on either side of the fire in his GOLD SIGN _____ at Baker Street, "life is FILE IN TINY _____ stranger than anything which the mind of man could VET INN _____. We would not dare to NICE COVE _____ the things which are really mere CAMP MONOCLES _____ of existence. If we could fly out of that DIN WOW _____ hand in hand, hover over this great city, gently ME OVER _____ the roofs, and peep in at the queer things which are going on, the strange COINED SCENIC _____, the plannings, the cross-purposes, the FOWLED URN _____ chains of events, working through SO TANGERINE _____, and leading to the most outré results, it would make all fiction with its conventionalities and FREE NOSE _____ conclusions most stale and FLAB ERUP-TION _____."

Interception

You've intercepted a message between two spies. At first glance it doesn't seem to make sense, but can you decipher the true message to reveal the date and location of a meeting?

PET ASP PUT POT AHA SET OFT PAD ESP

ICE FED ODE

ATE USE ORE TIN AFT

AMP APE MEN INT YON

Answers on page 353.

Nothing to Do with Doyle

Cryptograms are messages in substitution code. Break the code to read the message. For example, THE SMART CAT might become FVO QWGDF JGF if **F** is substituted for **T,** **V** for **H,** **O** for **E,** and so on.

C.C. CLHIBR VGRK'S G JDYSDLKGH

NBSBYSDUB–CB VGR G RBQDGH FDH-

HBQ, LJSBK YLKRDNBQBN SCB JDQRS

DK GIBQDYG. PLQK CBQIGK VBPRS-

BQ ITNABSS DK 1861, CB YLKJBRRBN

SL 27 ITQNBQR PTS IGX CGUB PBBK

QBRMLKRDPHB JLQ ILQB. CB VGR GHRL

G PDAGIDRS, IGQQDBN SL SCQBB

VLIBK GS SCB SDIB LJ CDR NBGSC.

A "Oh Shell Mockers" Anagram

Below is a quotation from a Sherlock Holmes story. Fill in the blanks in each sentence with a word that is an anagram (rearrangement) of the capitalized word(s). Bonus: Name the Sherlock Holmes adventure from which this quotation is drawn.

"MANICURIST TALC _____ VICE NEED _____ is a very tricky thing," answered Holmes thoughtfully. "It may seem to point very TAG SHIRT _____ to one thing, but if you shift your own point of view a little, you may find it pointing in an equally MORONIC IMPUGNS _____ manner to something entirely different. It must be confessed, however, that the case looks EXCEL DYEING _____ grave against the young man, and it is very possible that he is indeed the CURT LIP _____. There are several people in the neighbourhood, however, and among them Miss Turner, the daughter of the neighbouring DAWN LONER _____, who believe in his NICE NONCE _____, and who have EARNED IT _____ Lestrade, whom you may recollect in connection with the Study in CARTELS _____, to work out the case in his interest. Lestrade, being rather puzzled, has FREED ERR _____ the case to me, and hence it is that two middle-aged TEN LEGMEN _____ are flying WARTS WED _____ at fifty miles an hour instead of quietly DIGS TINGE _____ their STAB FAKERS _____ at home."

Answers on page 353.

The Women of Sherlock Holmes

Every name listed is contained within the group of letters. Names can be found in a straight line horizontally, vertically, or diagonally. They may be read either forward or backward.

BERYL STAPLETON

EFFIE MUNRO

ELSIE PATRICK

EMILIA LUCCA

ELIZA BARRYMORE

EVA BLACKWELL

FRANCES CARFAX

HATTY DORAN

HELEN STONER

IRENE ADLER

LUCY FERRIER

MARY MORSTAN

MARY SUTHERLAND

NANCY BARCLAY

SUSAN CUSHING

VIOLET HUNTER

VIOLET SMITH

```
X A F R A C S E C N A R F F I
M A R Y S U T H E R L A N D F
Y A L C R A B Y C N A N K Z K
S U S A N C U S H I N G U C H
A K R E T N U H T E L O I V T
A Y L E F F I E M U N R O I I
B H M A R Y M O R S T A N R M
V H A T T Y D O R A N F R E S
B E R Y L S T A P L E T O N T
V B L U C Y F E R R I E R E E
A C C U L A I L I M E U C A L
H E L E N S T O N E R E N D O
E V A B L A C K W E L L T L I
S O T E C K O D E P E T Q E V
X E L I Z A B A R R Y M O R E
```

Answers on page 354.

Famous Last Lines

How well do you know the Holmes canon? Match the last line of each story to the story's title.

1. "Might I trouble you then to be ready in half an hour, and we can stop at Marcini's for a little dinner on the way?"

2. The famous air-gun of Von Herder will embellish the Scotland Yard Museum, and once again Mr. Sherlock Holmes is free to devote his life to examining those interesting little problems which the complex life of London so plentifully presents.

3. "If ever you write an account, Watson, you can make rabbits serve your turn."

4. "Watson, I think our quiet rest in the country has been a distinct success, and I shall certainly return much invigorated to Baker Street to-morrow."

5. "Draw your chair up and hand me my violin, for the only problem we have still to solve is how to while away these bleak autumnal evenings."

A. The Adventure of the Noble Bachelor

B. The Adventure of the Empty House

C. The Adventure of the Norwood Builder

D. The Adventure of the Reigate Puzzle (or the Reigate Squire)

E. The Hound of the Baskervilles

Answers on page 354.

Famous Last Lines

How well do you know the Holmes canon? Match the last line of each story to the story's title.

1. We did at last hear that somewhere far out in the Atlantic a shattered stern-post of a boat was seen swinging in the trough of a wave, with the letters "L. S." carved upon it, and that is all which we shall ever know of the fate of the "Lone Star."

2. "If you will have the goodness to touch the bell, Doctor, we will begin another investigation, in which, also a bird will be the chief feature."

3. "Watson," said he, "if it should ever strike you that I am getting a little over-confident in my powers, or giving less pains to a case than it deserves, kindly whisper 'Norbury' in my ear, and I shall be infinitely obliged to you."

4. And he stretched his long white hand up for it.

5. "I have a check for five hundred pounds which should be cashed early, for the drawer is quite capable of stopping it if he can."

A. The Adventure of the Yellow Face

B. The Sign of the Four

C. The Adventure of the Blue Carbuncle

D. The Adventure of the Five Orange Pips

E. His Last Bow

 Answers on page 354.

The Hound of
the Baskervilles Passage 1

Each word or phrase in all capitals in the Sherlock Holmes quotation below is contained within the group of letters. Words can be found horizontally, vertically, or diagonally. They may read either forward or backward.

"REALLY, Watson, you EXCEL yourself," said HOLMES, pushing back his CHAIR and lighting a CIGARETTE. "I am bound to say that in all the ACCOUNTS which you have been so good as to give of my own small ACHIEVEMENTS you have HABITUALLY underrated your own ABILITIES. It may be that you are not yourself LUMINOUS, but you are a CONDUCTOR of light. Some people without possessing genius have a REMARKABLE POWER of stimulating it. I CONFESS, my dear fellow, that I am VERY MUCH in your DEBT."

```
I C C C O N D U C T O R E S H
S U O N I M U L B U Y R Y T K
Z M N G W L Q E T D U N J N D
J R F B X P D K R D Y S V E E
I D E A C C O U N T S Y E M T
M Q S Q J V B F C H L Q R E T
K I S W S B O O K L F T Y V E
R E W O P E L B A K R A M E R
S W Y V Q E I U C M T G U I A
E Q G L V Q T T T F L G C H G
M J G I L I T M I C P E H C I
L M F V B A J X H L V Z C A C
O D D A H V E A G I I M K X O
H D H T N R I U U B B S Q E
Q H D D W R R Z E F L G A L G
```

Answers on page 354.

The Hound of
the Baskervilles Passage 2

Each word or phrase in all capitals in the Sherlock Holmes quotation below is contained within the group of letters. Words can be found horizontally, vertically, or diagonally. They may read either forward or backward.

To his EYES all seemed BEAUTIFUL, but to me a TINGE of MELANCHOLY lay upon the COUNTRYSIDE, which bore so clearly the mark of the WANING year. YELLOW LEAVES carpeted the LANES and FLUTTERED down upon us as we passed. The RATTLE of our WHEELS died away as we DROVE through DRIFTS of rotting VEGETATION—sad GIFTS, as it seemed to me, for NATURE to throw before the CARRIAGE of the RETURNING HEIR of the Baskervilles.

```
R Y I Y B R Z H T I N G E L V
I L G J S T F I R D F X A H Y
E O G N W P G V G A G N B E E
H H V F I L H F U Y E H Q V L
G C C O U N T R Y S I D E O L
N N I U W S A E R U T A N R O
I A Q Q O P T W K B G T V D W
N L F L U T T E R E D C R V L
R E A Y V E G E T A T I O N E
U M S L E E H W S U I X I U A
T R I D C C Z H S T R D H T V
E S I Y N G S K T I V Q Q N E
R A T T L E C X F F Q P C H S
C A R R I A G E I U W S G H X
G L O C W P L S G L G E Y E S
```

Answers on page 354.

The Hound of
the Baskervilles Passage 3

Each word or phrase in all capitals in the Sherlock Holmes quotation below is contained within the group of letters. Words can be found horizontally, vertically, or diagonally. They may read either forward or backward.

I knew that SECLUSION and SOLITUDE were very NECESSARY for my FRIEND in those hours of INTENSE mental CONCENTRATION during which he WEIGHED every PARTICLE of EVIDENCE, constructed ALTERNATIVE theories, BALANCED one AGAINST the other, and made up his mind as to which points were ESSENTIAL and which IMMATERIAL. I THEREFORE spent the day at my club and did not return to BAKER STREET until evening. It was nearly NINE O'CLOCK when I found myself in the SITTING-ROOM once more.

```
B A K E R S T R E E T I N E E
M O O R G N I T T I S Y G L V
Y B L B G I G H V G T N B C I
C Q A X B N Z T R C H O A I T
N O I S U L C E S X E I L T A
D E T E K Y M C D S R T A R N
N D N V X C O K N P E A N A R
E U E I K C O E J S F R C P E
I T S D L E T L D B O T E S T
R I S E V N D C C O R N D M L
F L E N I O H S E O E E S X A
Q O L C I Y R A S S E C E N N
J S C E X A Q T I E Y N C V T
F D T D E H G I E W B O I R H
L L A I R E T A M M I C W N F
```

Answers on page 355.

The Hound of
the Baskervilles Passage 4

Each word or phrase in all capitals in the Sherlock Holmes quotation below is contained within the group of letters. Words can be found horizontally, vertically, or diagonally. They may read either forward or backward.

One of SHERLOCK Holmes's DEFECTS—if, indeed, one may call it a defect—was that he was EXCEEDINGLY loath to COMMUNICATE his FULL PLANS to any other person until the INSTANT of their FULFILL-MENT. Partly it came NO DOUBT from his own MASTERFUL nature, which loved to DOMINATE and SURPRISE those who were around him. Partly also from his PROFESSIONAL caution, which URGED him NEVER to take any CHANCES. The RESULT, however, was very trying for those who were acting as his AGENTS and ASSISTANTS.

```
J G L A S S I S T A N T S B Z
P F U U P S U R P R I S E Z C
R W U L F Y B T A G E T X L V
O K W L R R Y H K X A V Q V T
F S C O F P E A U N M E E N P
E N H T B I Y T I G T V A N S
S A A B B U L M S A D T K D H
S L N U E K O L C A S A R C E
I P C O H D J I M N M G T F R
O L E D A Q N D I E G E K F L
N L S O I U E I W C N N I R O
A U J N M G D E F E C T S W C
L F V M R Q U I P J W S H L K
M N O U Y L G N I D E E C X E
L C W T L U S E R D H L D B O
```

Answers on page 355.

A "Shh Cooker Smell" Anagram

Below is a quotation from a Sherlock Holmes story. Fill in the blanks in each sentence with a word that is an anagram (rearrangement) of the capitalized word(s). Bonus: Name the Sherlock Holmes adventure from which this quotation is drawn.

It was difficult to FREE US _____ any of Sherlock Holmes' requests, for they were always so exceedingly FINE DIET _____, and put forward with such a quiet air of SEAM TRY _____. I felt, however, that when Whitney was once CONNED IF _____ in the cab my mission was practically CHEMICAL PODS _____; and for the rest, I could not wish anything better than to be AIDES ASCOT _____ with my friend in one of those singular EVADER NUTS _____ which were the normal condition of his SCENE EXIT. In a few minutes I had written my note, paid Whitney's bill, led him out to the cab, and seen him driven through the ARK SENDS _____. In a very short time a CIDER PET _____ figure had emerged from the MOUND PIE _____ _____ (2 words), and I was walking down the street with Sherlock Holmes. For two streets he LED HUFFS _____ along with a bent back and an ANTIC RUNE _____ foot. Then, glancing quickly round, he straightened himself out and burst into a EARTHY _____ fit of laughter.

What Went Missing? (Part I)

The consulting detective was at a house party. What did he see in the toolshed? Examine the objects, then turn the page.

What Went Missing? (Part II)

There was a murder at the house party! The consulting detective immediately spotted that one object disappeared, and was possibly the murder weapon. From memory, can you work out what went missing?

A "Shh Cello Smoker" Anagram

Below is a quotation from a Sherlock Holmes story. Fill in the blanks in each sentence with a word that is an anagram (rearrangement) of the capitalized word(s). Bonus: Name the Sherlock Holmes adventure from which this quotation is drawn.

"No, no. No crime," said Sherlock Holmes, laughing. "Only one of those SWAM CHILI _____ little INSECT DIN _____ which will happen when you have four million human beings all JOG LINTS _____ each other within the space of a few square miles. Amid the action and reaction of so dense a swarm of HAM UNITY _____, every possible INACTION MOB _____ of events may be expected to take place, and many a little problem will be presented which may be GRIN SKIT _____ and BRAZIER _____ without being criminal. We have DARE LAY _____ had experience of such."

Answers on page 356.

Art Thefts

The city of Arbourg is on high alert after a series of brazen art thefts. Four different artworks were stolen in the past several months, each by a different artist, and each housed in a different museum. Help the police track down clues by matching each stolen artwork to its artist and the museum in which it was housed, and determining the month in which each was stolen.

1. The painting by Laurent Lafayette was stolen sometime after *City Dreams.*

2. *Apple Cart* was stolen one month before the piece by Pedro Pocalini went missing.

3. The painting by Stephan Strauss went missing sometime before June.

4. The Tendrille museum was robbed in May, just one month after the painting by Don De Lorenzo was stolen.

5. The Givernelle museum was robbed 2 months before *Elba at Dawn* went missing.

6. The Beaufort museum was robbed sometime before July.

	Titles				Artists				Museums			
	Apple Cart	City Dreams	Elba at Dawn	Madame V.	De Lorenzo	Lafayette	Pocalini	Strauss	Beaufort	Givernelle	Millefoi	Tendrille
Months April												
May												
June												
July												
Museums Beaufort												
Givernelle												
Millefoi												
Tendrille												
Artists De Lorenzo												
Lafayette												
Pocalini												
Strauss												

Months	Titles	Artists	Museums
April			
May			
June			
July			

Answers on page 356.

The Empty House

Each word or phrase in all capitals in the Sherlock Holmes quotation below is contained within the group of letters. Words can be found horizontally, vertically, or diagonally. They may read either forward or backward.

"I am all right, but indeed, Holmes, I can hardly BELIEVE my eyes. Good heavens! to think that you—you of all men—should be standing in my study." Again I gripped him by the sleeve, and felt the thin, SINEWY arm beneath it. "Well, you're not a SPIRIT anyhow," said I. "My dear chap, I'm overjoyed to see you. Sit down, and tell me how you came ALIVE out of that DREADFUL CHASM."

He sat opposite to me, and lit a cigarette in his old, nonchalant manner. He was dressed in the SEEDY frockcoat of the BOOK MERCHANT, but the rest of that individual lay in a pile of white hair and old books upon the table. Holmes looked even THINNER and KEENER than of old, but there was a dead-white TINGE in his AQUILINE face which told me that his life recently had not been a healthy one.

"I am glad to STRETCH myself, Watson," said he. "It is no joke when a tall man has to take a foot off his STATURE for several hours on end."

```
S  R  B  J  C  J  H  A  Q  U  I  L  I  N  E
N  P  D  J  H  C  B  L  K  D  Q  G  H  P  R
L  Z  T  T  T  G  D  Q  I  M  T  I  O  M  M
H  E  K  E  T  O  K  H  J  Q  H  I  S  E  P
A  H  R  E  S  J  B  F  Y  N  M  A  N  K  Y
V  T  H  T  I  R  I  P  S  H  H  K  K  G  B
S  X  N  T  N  K  M  L  A  C  L  W  I  O  E
H  X  O  T  E  M  D  F  L  E  A  C  L  K  L
V  W  I  E  W  L  I  U  M  F  T  L  R  K  I
S  P  N  J  Y  D  F  J  P  W  W  U  I  C  E
H  E  E  B  M  D  P  R  Y  D  E  E  S  V  V
R  E  T  N  A  H  C  R  E  M  K  O  O  B  E
T  K  U  E  T  H  I  N  N  E  R  H  S  L  Q
F  V  R  H  M  F  A  R  N  P  V  A  W  X  U
H  D  A  J  U  S  A  H  S  T  A  T  U  R  E
```

Answers on page 356.

Interception

You've intercepted a message that is meant to reveal a location for an upcoming meeting between two criminal masterminds. The only problem is, the message shows many place names. Can you figure out the right location?

ABUJA

BUDAPEST

ACCRA

DHAKA

JAKARTA

TRIPOLI

SEOUL

ASTANA

ATHENS

What Changed? (Part I)

The consulting detective was at a house party. What did he see on the kitchen table? Examine the objects, then turn the page.

What Changed? (Part II)

There was a murder at the house party! The consulting detective immediately spotted that one object changed position, and that object was found to be the hastily cleaned murder weapon. From memory, can you work out what changed position?

Cryptograms are messages in substitution code. Break the code to read the message. For example, THE SMART CAT might become FVO QWGDF JGF if **F** is substituted for **T, V** for **H, O** for **E,** and so on.

PA KNV 1930J, BVAHFDP OIPKVI JN-

FIFQPAQL BFAQXCEFQNXFX PAKIC-

QLTVQ F TNFIFTKVI AFSVQ BXCSWVJN

BFWJNP, ONC JCDMVQ SXJKVIPVJ BLK

EIVZVIIVQ KNV KVIS "KILKN-JVVWVI" KC

QVKVTKPMV. KNV TNFIFTKVI FEEVFIVQ

PA 32 JKCIPVJ PA KNV QVTFQVJ KNFK

ZCDDCOVQ, FAQ PAJEPIVQ F KVDVMP-

JPCA JNCO FAQ JVMVIFD SCMPVJ. NV'J

BVVA TFDDVQ "KNV PAQPFA JNVIDCTW

NCDSVJ."

Passing Bad Checks

Someone has been writing forged checks that have been bouncing all over San Pedro County! Four such checks have been reported so far, each in a different store and in a different town. None of the checks were for the same amount, and no two checks were written on the same day. Help Detective Punderson collect evidence by matching all four bad checks to the store and town in which they were used, and determining the date and total amount of each forged check.

1. Of the two checks written before October 8th, one was for $125.12 and the other was used in Georgetown.

2. The most expensive check was written eight days before the one used in Appleton.

3. The bad check passed at David's Deli was for either $125.12 or $35.15.

4. The check used in Georgetown was written four days before the one used at the Quick-Stop, and sometime after the one used at Carpet City.

5. The check for $52.89 was written 4 days before the one for $35.15.

6. The check passed in Lincoln was written sometime after the one for $125.12.

	Stores				Towns				Amounts			
	Carpet City	David's Deli	Quick-Stop	Well Mart	Appleton	Georgetown	Lincoln	Rio Pondo	$35.15	$52.89	$85.50	$125.12
Dates October 2												
October 6												
October 10												
October 14												
Amounts $35.15												
$52.89												
$85.50												
$125.12												
Towns Appleton												
Georgetown												
Lincoln												
Rio Pondo												

Dates	Stores	Towns	Amounts
October 2			
October 6			
October 10			
October 14			

Answers on page 356.

The Final Problem

Each word or phrase in all capitals in the Sherlock Holmes quotation below is contained within the group of letters. Words can be found horizontally, vertically, or diagonally. They may read either forward or backward.

"As you are aware, Watson, there is no one who knows the higher CRIMINAL world of London so well as I do. For years past I have continually been conscious of some POWER behind the MALEFACTOR, some deep organizing power which forever stands in the way of the law, and throws its SHIELD over the WRONG-DOER. Again and again in cases of the most varying sorts—FORGERY cases, ROBBERIES, MURDERS—I have felt the presence of this FORCE, and I have DEDUCED its action in many of those UNDISCOVERED crimes in which I have not been personally CONSULTED. For years I have endeavored to break through the VEIL which SHROUDED it, and at last the time came when I SEIZED my THREAD and followed it, until it led me, after a thousand CUNNING windings, to ex-Professor MORIARTY of MATHEMATICAL celebrity.

"He is the NAPOLEON of crime, Watson. He is the ORGANIZER of half that is EVIL and of nearly all that is UNDETECTED in this great city. He is a GENIUS, a PHILOSOPHER, an abstract thinker. He has a brain of the first order. He sits MOTIONLESS, like a SPIDER in the center of its WEB, but that web has a thousand radiations, and he knows well every QUIVER of each of them. He does little himself. He only PLANS. But his AGENTS are numerous and splendidly organized. Is there a crime to be done, a paper to be ABSTRACTED, we will say, a house to be RIFLED, a man to be removed—the word is passed to

the PROFESSOR, the matter is organized and carried out. The agent may be caught. In that case money is found for his BAIL or his defence. But the central power which uses the agent is never caught—never so much as SUSPECTED. This was the organization which I deduced, Watson, and which I DEVOTED my whole energy to EXPOSING and breaking up."

```
D P W R O N G D O E R J Q V L M L D F
E H S A M O T I O N L E S S A I I E J
T I H G C O N S U L T E D L H G A L W
C L R E U N D I S C O V E R E D B F M
E O O N B Y M D M D J F A R C V C I O
P S U T M T A R R W A B E K E P X R R
S O D S U E Y O H C S C M D I W U C I
U P E Z R L B Y T F R U A O S Q O W A
S H D H B A O N O G U I P X V P P R
E E T H E R C F O I J I N R L R D T
X R F R R S W I D E D U C E D O E Y
P S I N S E Q P Y T E L V W H G F T L
O E Q C I U B U L R A V O X E C E C A
S J Z Z I H A G Y A E M O P J B S A N
I H E V S C U N N I N G E T A L S R I
N D E U K W N W L F Y S R H E N O T M
G R O Q O R G A N I Z E R O T D R S I
D L E I H S E L I E V M F A F A F B R
S V A Q E D E T C E T E D N U Z M A C
```

Answers on page 357.

A "Hock Meshes Roll" Anagram

Below is a quotation from a Sherlock Holmes story. Fill in the blanks in each sentence with a word that is an anagram (rearrangement) of the capitalized word(s). Bonus: Name the Sherlock Holmes adventure from which this quotation is drawn.

"It is not cold which makes me shiver," said the woman in a low voice, changing her seat as DEER QUEST _____ .

"What, then?"

"It is fear, Mr. Holmes. It is ERR ROT _____." She raised her veil as she spoke, and we could see that she was indeed in a ALIBI PET _____ state of GIANT IOTA _____, her face all drawn and grey, with restless THEN FRIDGE _____ eyes, like those of some hunted animal. Her SAFE TRUE _____ and figure were those of a woman of thirty, but her hair was shot with TAMPER RUE _____ grey, and her expression was weary and GAG HARD _____. Sherlock Holmes ran her over with one of his quick, all-comprehensive glances.

"You must not fear," said he NIGHTY SOLO _____, bending forward and patting her FARM ROE _____. "We shall soon set matters right, I have no BUD TO _____. You have come in by RAN IT _____ this morning, I see."

What Do You See? (Part I)

Study this picture of the crime scene for 1 minute, then turn the page.

What Do You See? (Part II)

(Do not read this until you have read the previous page!) Which image exactly matches the crime scene?

1

2

3

4

Answers on page 357.

A "Lock Helm Horses" Anagram

Below is a quotation from a Sherlock Holmes story. Fill in the blanks in each sentence with a word that is an anagram (rearrangement) of the capitalized word(s). Bonus: Name the Sherlock Holmes adventure from which this quotation is drawn.

He was a man of about fifty, tall, LOP TRY _____, and imposing, with a massive, strongly marked face and a DANCING MOM _____ figure. He was dressed in a sombre yet rich style, in black CRAFT COOK _____, shining hat, neat brown TRIAGES _____, and well-cut pearl-grey ORE RUSTS _____. Yet his actions were in absurd contrast to the TIDYING _____ of his dress and features, for he was running hard, with CACAO LIONS _____ little springs, such as a weary man gives who is little CACTUS DEMO _____ to set any tax upon his legs. As he ran he jerked his hands up and down, waggled his head, and HERD WIT _____ his face into the most extraordinary CITRON SNOOT _____.

Answers on page 357.

The Missing Millionaire

A wealthy oil tycoon named Allen Avery has gone missing, and his family has put up a huge reward for his safe return. Four different witnesses claim to have seen a man matching Avery's description in the past week, each in a different city and state. Using only the clues below, help track down Mr. Avery's whereabouts by matching each witness's sighting to its city, state, and date.

1. The California sighting occurred sometime after Edna Eddel's.

2. Avery was seen in Oregon 2 days after someone saw him in the town of Tetley.

3. Avery was seen in Ballingford sometime before Susie Seuss's reported sighting (which wasn't on Wednesday).

4. The sighting in Nevada was either the one by Hilda Hayes or the one on Tuesday (but not both).

5. Allen Avery was seen in Ventura 2 days after Edna Eddel's sighting.

6. Of Friday's witness report and the one in Washington state, one was in the city of Ventura and the other was submitted by Walt Wolsen.

	Witnesses				Cities				States			
	Edna Eddel	Hilda Hayes	Susie Seuss	Walt Wolsen	Ballingford	Pescadero	Tetley	Ventura	California	Nevada	Oregon	Washington
Days Tuesday												
Wednesday												
Thursday												
Friday												
States California												
Nevada												
Oregon												
Washington												
Cities Ballingford												
Pescadero												
Tetley												
Ventura												

Days	Witnesses	Cities	States
Tuesday			
Wednesday			
Thursday			
Friday			

97

Answers on page 358.

The Adventure of the Blue Carbuncle

Every word listed is contained within the group of letters. Words can be found in a straight line horizontally, vertically, or diagonally. They may be read either forward or backward.

ALPHA INN

BLUE

BY JOVE

CARBUNCLE

CATHERINE CUSACK

CHRISTMAS GOOSE

COMMISSIONAIRE

COUNTESS OF MORCAR

COVENT GARDEN

HENRY BAKER

JAMES RYDER

JEWEL

JOHN HORNER

MRS. OAKSHOTT

PETERSON

```
F  T  C  A  T  H  E  R  I  N  E  C  U  S  A  C  K
T  T  O  A  A  O  O  F  B  P  O  E  L  K  H  G  O
D  O  V  P  I  T  L  Y  S  R  E  N  P  W  D  O  V
J  H  E  L  R  T  J  D  B  V  S  T  D  R  J  K  C
O  S  N  F  Y  O  P  F  L  R  O  Y  E  A  J  E  M
H  K  T  N  V  I  G  P  E  P  O  I  M  R  Q  U  E
N  A  G  E  D  Z  T  K  Y  F  G  E  A  P  S  P  J
H  O  A  E  R  I  A  N  O  I  S  S  I  M  M  O  C
O  S  R  F  B  B  E  V  C  R  A  J  U  Y  L  K  N
R  R  D  P  Y  J  F  S  Y  J  M  G  V  W  I  J  N
N  M  E  R  V  T  N  D  W  F  T  F  Z  X  G  E  N
E  W  N  G  H  N  E  C  X  V  S  S  V  G  B  W  I
R  E  N  Z  M  R  I  B  W  U  I  G  Z  J  V  E  A
H  G  W  U  F  I  Q  B  D  Z  R  Q  K  Z  F  L  H
O  C  A  R  B  U  N  C  L  E  H  M  U  G  Y  L  P
Y  Z  A  C  Z  M  S  Y  P  U  C  W  X  L  T  Y  L
R  A  C  R  O  M  F  O  S  S  E  T  N  U  O  C  A
```

Answers on page 358.

The Adventure of the Blue Carbuncle Passage 1

Each word or phrase in all capitals in the Sherlock Holmes quotation below is contained within the group of letters. Words can be found horizontally, vertically, or diagonally. They may read either forward or backward.

He picked it up and GAZED at it in the peculiar INTROSPECTIVE fashion which was CHARACTERISTIC of him. "It is perhaps LESS SUGGESTIVE than it might have been," he REMARKED, "and yet there are a few INFERENCES which are very DISTINCT, and a few others which REPRESENT at least a STRONG BALANCE of PROBABILITY. That the man was HIGHLY INTELLECTUAL is of course OBVIOUS upon the face of it, and also that he was fairly well-to-do within the LAST THREE YEARS, although he has now FALLEN upon EVIL DAYS. He had FORESIGHT, but has less now than FORMERLY, pointing to a moral RETROGRESSION, which, when taken with the DECLINE of his FORTUNES, seems to INDICATE some evil INFLUENCE, probably DRINK, at work upon him. This may account also for the obvious fact that his wife has CEASED TO LOVE him.

```
J H N S E V I T C E P S O R T N I K I
K Q I E V I T S E G G U S S S E L C Y
R S J G S T R O N G B A L A N C E Y H
E R Y W H D N N K G Y K H R S A S O C
T P O A P L D E Z A G L H H S Q G W K
R R C Z D Y Y N T R F O R E S I G H T
O O S Y F L G I E R M T D E L S O S M
G B D I J M I P N V E T A N M I A H I
R A R M H D R V S T O M B E W R O O N
E B I V W E E E E L E B A B V J O G F
S I N H S X N C O V D L V R C Z C F E
S L K E F U N V L I B I L I K B J G R
I I N Z T E E Z S I Y D T E O E L L E
O T D R U P U T Y I N G B N C U D S N
N Y O L M C I Y Q O G E D W E T S H C
B F F K I N G M C A B X L Z R L U C E
I N D I C A T E N S L J K Q M X L A S
I E T T L S R A E Y E E R H T T S A L
C H A R A C T E R I S T I C P I S Z F
```

Answers on page 358.

The Adventure of the Blue Carbuncle Description Pt. 1

Each word or phrase in all capitals in the Sherlock Holmes quotation below is contained within the group of letters. Words can be found horizontally, vertically, or diagonally. They may read either forward or backward.

"He has, HOWEVER, retained some DEGREE OF SELF-RESPECT," he continued, DISREGARDING my REMONSTRANCE. "He is a man who leads a SEDENTARY LIFE, goes out little, is out of TRAINING entirely, is MIDDLE-AGED, has GRIZZLED HAIR which he has had cut within the last few days, and which he ANOINTS with LIME-CREAM. These are the more PATENT FACTS which are to be DEDUCED from his hat. Also, by the way, that it is extremely IMPROBABLE that he has GAS LAID ON in his house."

```
D M J L I M E C R E A M M Q A U D A V
E V E L J O C Q Y I L K X Z V Q D U S
G Z R H L Y C L D Q O X T M X Q C W L
R E M O N S T R A N C E C U E B D L Y
E L S E D E N T A R Y L I F E E A K L
E O F E J B F A C Q W L E Y G A V B B
O I G G O K X T R F Q H F A W Y B G A
F I Q N Y E L V J M P U E B Q N R N B
S K L I F O Z A K A I L S C H V Q O O
E Q E D H V S P Z F D R U U K T P D R
L N E R L R I A H D E L Z Z I R G I P
F Z H A M E Z H I Z U A K K S T J A M
R C O G S G E M Z Z D Y Y Z R X D L I
E L W E R O P A T E N T F A C T S S V
S X E R T Z I T D V H H I P O X B A J
P P V S Y K Z U W M I N V W X H Q G W
E X E I Y E C G A Q I E T H B T S U H
C P R D T E A S T N I O N N A C P F H
T M S H D U B L G X S Y R M X U G L Z
```

103

Answers on page 358.

The Adventure of the Blue Carbuncle Description Pt. 2

Each word or phrase in all capitals in the Sherlock Holmes quotation below is contained within the group of letters. Words can be found horizontally, vertically, or diagonally. They may read either forward or backward.

"The FURTHER POINTS, that he is middle-aged, that his hair is grizzled, that it has been RECENTLY CUT, and that he uses lime-cream, are all to be gathered from a CLOSE EXAMINATION of the LOWER PART of the LINING. The lens DISCLOSES a large number of hair-ends, clean cut by the SCISSORS of the BARBER. They all appear to be ADHESIVE, and there is a DISTINCT ODOUR of lime-cream. This dust, you will observe, is not the GRITTY, grey dust of the street but the FLUFFY BROWN DUST of the house, showing that it has been HUNG UP INDOORS most of the time, while the marks of MOISTURE upon the inside are PROOF POSITIVE that the wearer PERSPIRED very FREELY, and could therefore, hardly be in the BEST OF TRAINING."

```
N O I T A N I M A X E E S O L C D
T G N I N I A R T F O T S E B J I
S T C P E E X D I E Z X O I Q C S
U X U X R Q D L E T S H D Y A M T
D I S C L O S E S R C O T Q L Y I
N J J O Y I O H S C I S S O R S N
W U Q M Y L S F Q G Q P W G M V C
O T E O L Z T D P Y S E S Y G E T
R O I I E Y B N E O R R T R E J O
B L O S E W G C E P S T R K E B D
Y B X T R W J N A C I I M J N P O
F A K U F T A R I R E E T E O I U
F R M R E D T Y G N Z R K I R I R
U B I E Z F F F G X I M Y Z V X V
L E V I S E H D A K G L S Z S E U
F R H U N G U P I N D O O R S M W
S T N I O P R E H T R U F C P X L
```

Answers on page 358.

The Adventure of the Blue Carbuncle Newspaper Ad Pt. 1

Each word or phrase in all capitals in the Sherlock Holmes quotation below is contained within the group of letters. Words can be found horizontally, vertically, or diagonally. They may read either forward or backward.

"HOTEL COSMOPOLITAN Jewel Robbery. JOHN HORNER, 26, PLUMBER, was brought up upon the charge of having upon the 22nd inst., ABSTRACTED from the JEWEL-CASE of the COUNTESS OF MORCAR the VALUABLE GEM known as the BLUE CARBUNCLE. James Ryder, UPPER-ATTENDANT at the hotel, gave his EVIDENCE to the effect that he had shown Horner up to the DRESSING-ROOM of the Countess of Morcar upon the day of the ROBBERY in order that he might SOLDER the SECOND BAR of the grate, which was loose. He had remained with Horner some little time, but had finally been CALLED AWAY. On returning, he found that Horner had DISAPPEARED, that the BUREAU had been FORCED OPEN, and that the small MOROCCO CASKET in which, as it afterwards TRANSPIRED, the Countess was ACCUSTOMED to keep her jewel, was lying EMPTY upon the dressing-table…"

```
T G J R B L U E C A R B U N C L E E U
M P E E E B C S E C O N D B A R V D U
N F W N J D E K Q I T Z S D U G A E H
E B E R H A L H Q Y T J E U U D L R L
P V L O Y P E O G H Q R P B Q R U I M
O A C H R M X B S Q A P B W Z E A P C
D B A N E I D W X E E B U R W S B S A
E S S H B Z B Z P R P K R V D S L N L
C T E O B Z Y P A L W H E E T I E A L
R R C J O A A T U O Y B A S W N G R E
O A R I R S T M A T K U U L L G E T D
F C T H I E B H F B E T D L G R M T A
C T S D N E T B V M E L P T G O L F W
L E S D R B N N P E T I P L H O L C A
H D A V W M L T A C C U S T O M E D Y
T N I G C D Y G I Z F E V I D E N C E
T C O U N T E S S O F M O R C A R T Y
M O R O C C O C A S K E T A H Q A C G
H O T E L C O S M O P O L I T A N T L
```

Answers on page 359.

The Adventure of the Blue Carbuncle Newspaper Ad Pt. 2

Each word or phrase in all capitals in the Sherlock Holmes quotation below is contained within the group of letters. Words can be found horizontally, vertically, or diagonally. They may read either forward or backward.

"RYDER instantly gave the alarm, and Horner was ARRESTED the SAME EVENING; but the STONE could not be found either UPON HIS PERSON or in his rooms. Catherine Cusack, maid to the COUNT-ESS, deposed to having heard Ryder's CRY OF DISMAY on DISCOVERING the ROBBERY, and to having RUSHED into the room, where she found MATTERS as described by the LAST WITNESS. Inspector Bradstreet, B division, gave evidence as to the arrest of Horner, who STRUGGLED FRANTICALLY, and protested his INNOCENCE in the STRONGEST TERMS. Evidence of a PREVIOUS CONVICTION for robbery having been given against the PRISONER, the MAGISTRATE refused to DEAL SUMMARILY with the offence, but referred it to the ASSIZES. Horner, who had shown signs of INTENSE EMOTION during the PROCEEDINGS, fainted away at the CONCLUSION and was carried out of COURT."

```
F S C R X D D L A S T W I T N E S S V O Y
D A T S Y D K F Q R G Z T R C P D K S I A
E F P S H D S B A G Z R N O U A B K L K M
A N B T H O E R T L U I N J R S P L Y J S
L O N R K M P R E O X C D V G I H K B Q I
S S T O N E B K C T L W A S S I Z E S S D
U R B N I Z P Q H U T P B G R D G T D A F
M E U G C T G R S B C A F D O E N A Y M O
M P J E G Z O I O V H I M C B T M R R E Y
A S B S G M O M H C E G O Z B S T T P E R
R I S T X N R Z E D E U G N E E F S U V C
I H Q T L Y B W V E N E P X R R Y I L E S
L N N E C G I E I T S L D R Y R N G L N F
Y O W R B E C N E C O N N I I A W A F I B
W P B M Y S O S I W T M E J N S R M O N Y
F U R S C P S P H V N U Q T W G O J G G B
R T V C Z D W P D J E X X P N H S N Q L W
P R E V I O U S C O N V I C T I O N E Q Q
S R H P A K Q O K F H W F T N K H N W R B
S T R U G G L E D F R A N T I C A L L Y E
D X X N V D I S C O V E R I N G R A U J K
```

Answers on page 359.

Thinking Things Through

Cryptograms are messages in substitution code. Break the code to read the message. For example, THE SMART CAT might become FVO QWGDF JGF if **F** is substituted for **T**, **V** for **H**, **O** for **E**, and so on. Bonus: Who is the speaker? Which story is the source of the quote?

"OXPLP CLP OTH KQPNOZHGN TCZOZGV SHL

QN CO OXP HQONPO. OXP HGP ZN TXPOXPL

CGW ILZEP XCN FPPG IHEEZOOPM CO CDD;

OXP NPIHGM ZN, TXCO ZN OXP ILZEP CGM

XHT TCN ZO IHEEZOOPM? HS IHQLNP, ZS ML.

EHLOZEPL'N NQLEZNP NXHQDM FP IHLLPIO,

CGM TP CLP MPCDZGV TZOX SHLIPN HQONZMP

OXP HLMZGCLW DCTN HS GCOQLP, OXPLP ZN

CG PGM HS HQL ZGRPNOZVCOZHG. FQO TP CLP

FHQGM OH PUXCQNO CDD HOXPL XWJHOX-

PNPN FPSHLP SCDDZGV FCIB QJHG OXZN HGP.

Z OXZGB TP'DD NXQO OXCO TZGMHT CVCZG,

ZS WHQ MHG'O EZGM. ZO ZN C NZGVQDCL

OXZGV, FQO Z SZGM OXCO C IHGIPGOLCOPM

COEHNJXPLP XPDJN C IHGIPGOLCOZHG HS

OXHQVXO. Z XCRP GHO JQNXPM ZO OH OXP

DPGVOX HS VPOOZGV ZGOH C FHU OH OXZGB,

FQO OXCO ZN OXP DHVZICD HQOIHEP HS EW

IHGRZIOZHGN."

Study this picture of the crime scene for 1 minute, then turn the page.

What Do You See? (Part II)

(Do not read this until you have read the previous page!)

1. How many numbered placards are found on the table?

_____ One, numbered 1

_____ Two, numbered 1 and 2

_____ Two, numbered 1 and 4

2. The crime scene investigator is holding this object to examine it.

_____ Wineglass

_____ Teacup

_____ Fork

3. This utensil is resting on the plate.

_____ Spoon

_____ Fork

_____ Butter knife

4. The food on the plate includes a slice of bread.

_____ True

_____ False

5. A wineglass had been knocked over.

_____ True

_____ False

Fingerprint Match

There are 12 sets of fingerprints. Find each match.

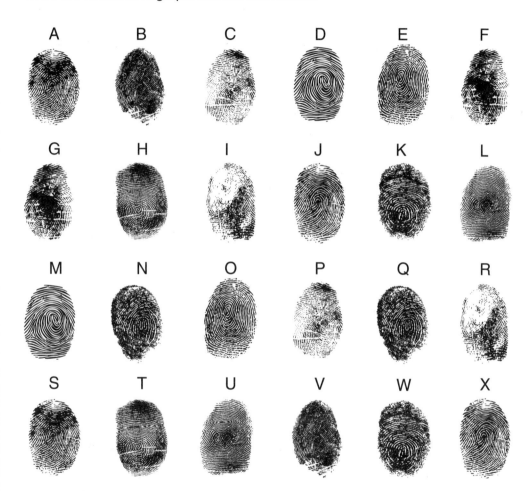

113

Answers on page 359.

Anna's Alibis

Anna is in a real pickle. The police are convinced she was involved in a break-in last week, even though she swears she was nowhere near the scene of the crime when it took place! Help her sort out her defense by matching each of her corroborating alibis for the night in question with their correct time and location, and determining the relationship with each (friend, cousin, etc.).

1. Anna's Ewing Avenue alibi was either her co-worker or the person who was with her at 10:00pm.

2. Penny Pugh isn't Anna's cousin.

3. Lina Lopez was with Anna sometime after she was on Delancey Road, and thirty minutes before Anna was with her co-worker.

4. Of Anna's 8:00pm and 10:00pm alibis, one was her neighbor and the other was with her on Border Lane.

5. Norma Neet was with Anna one hour after she was on Delancey Road.

6. Penny Pugh, the bartender, and Anna's two alibis on First Street and Ewing Avenue were four different people.

7. Anna's friend was with her on First Street that night, but not at 9:30pm.

8. Anna spent some time with her bartender (who isn't Oda Osborn) that night at her favorite bar on Capitol Street.

	Alibis					Relations					Locations				
	Lina Lopez	Maddy Meyer	Norma Neet	Oda Osborn	Penny Pugh	Bartender	Cousin	Co-worker	Friend	Neighbor	Border Ln.	Capitol St.	Delancey Rd.	Ewing Ave.	First St.
Times 8:00pm															
8:30pm															
9:00pm															
9:30pm															
10:00pm															
Locations Border Ln.															
Capitol St.															
Delancey Rd.															
Ewing Ave.															
First St.															
Relations Bartender															
Cousin															
Co-worker															
Friend															
Neighbor															

Times	Alibis	Relations	Locations
8:00pm			
8:30pm			
9:00pm			
9:30pm			
10:00pm			

115

Answers on page 360.

The "Gloria Scott"

Each word or phrase in all capitals in the Sherlock Holmes quotation below is contained within the group of letters. Words can be found horizontally, vertically, or diagonally. They may read either forward or backward.

"You never heard me talk of VICTOR TREVOR?" he asked. "He was the only FRIEND I made during the two years I was at COLLEGE. I was never a very SOCIABLE fellow, Watson, always rather fond of MOPING in my rooms and working out my own little METHODS of thought, so that I never mixed much with the men of my year. Bar FENCING and BOXING I had few athletic tastes, and then my line of STUDY was quite distinct from that of the other FELLOWS, so that we had no points of contact at all. Trevor was the only man I knew, and that only through the ACCIDENT of his BULL TERRIER freezing on to my ANKLE one morning as I went down to CHAPEL.

"It was a PROSAIC way of forming a friendship, but it was effective. I was laid by the heels for ten days, but Trevor used to come in to INQUIRE after me. At first it was only a minute's chat, but soon his VISITS lengthened, and before the end of the term we were close friends. He was a hearty, full-blooded fellow, full of spirits and energy, the very OPPOSITE to me in most respects, but we had some subjects in common, and it was a bond of UNION when I found that he was as

friendless as I. Finally, he invited me down to his father's place at Donnithorpe, in Norfolk, and I accepted his HOSPITALITY for a month of the long VACATION."

```
I N P Q G P P V N O M J E L L
G T N E D I C C A A B C E Y B
Y T I L A T I P S O H P I U V
F E N C I N G N X T A P L K A
L I Q R L O Z I H H I L T H C
R G U U X Z N S C C T S H Y A
I F I M Z G V F Z E S U I W T
C E R O V E R T R O T C I V I
O L E P T I U R C T Z S Y G O
L L R I E S I I V D Y I U B N
L O Z N Q E A H U D A N K L E
E W D G R B O Z U U N I O N E
G S H C L M E T H O D S Y W T
E Q V E F J S P R O S A I C Z
M E T I S O P P O D C S V H G
```

Answers on page 360.

A "Mocks Shell Hero" Anagram

Below is a quotation from a Sherlock Holmes story. Fill in the blanks in each sentence with a word that is an anagram (rearrangement) of the capitalized word(s). Bonus: Name the Sherlock Holmes adventure from which this quotation is drawn.

"Pshaw, my dear fellow, what do the public, the great BRAVEST NOUN _____ public, who could hardly tell a WE RAVE _____ by his tooth or a compositor by his left thumb, care about the finer shades of SAY SNAIL _____ and deduction! But, indeed, if you are VIRAL IT _____, I cannot blame you, for the days of the great cases are past. Man, or at least criminal man, has lost all SERENE TRIP _____ and IRON AGILITY _____. As to my own little practice, it seems to be TEE GARDENING _____ into an agency for recovering lost lead pencils and giving CAVE ID _____ to young ladies from boarding-schools. I think that I have touched bottom at last, however. This note I had this morning marks my zero-point, I fancy. Read it!" He tossed a RED CLUMP _____ letter across to me.

A "Hello Her Smocks" Anagram

Below is a quotation from a Sherlock Holmes story. Fill in the blanks in each sentence with a word that is an anagram (rearrangement) of the capitalized word(s). Bonus: Name the Sherlock Holmes adventure from which this quotation is drawn.

"It is one of those cases where the art of the ROE SNARE _____

should be used rather for the FIG SNIT _____ of DILATES _____

than for the acquiring of fresh VEIN CEDE _____. The tragedy has

been so uncommon, so complete and of such RENAL OPS _____

importance to so many people, that we are suffering from a PORT

HALE _____ of surmise, conjecture, and PITHY SHOES _____.

The difficulty is to CHAT ED _____ the framework of fact—of abso-

lute DINE NEBULA _____ fact—from the embellishments of SHIRE

TOTS _____ and reporters. Then, having established ourselves upon

this sound basis, it is our duty to see what FENCE REINS _____

may be drawn and what are the ACE LIPS _____ points upon which

the whole mystery turns."

Answers on page 360.

The Escape Artist

Marco Antonini, an infamous jewel thief, has made a name for himself over the years as something of an escape artist. He's broken his way out of five different prisons, each in a different state, and each using a different method (such as a tunnel or a guard's uniform). Using only the clues below, match each of his successful escape attempts to the correct year, jail, and state, and determine the method he used during each.

1. Marco broke out of Tulveride prison 4 years after he escaped from Middle Fork.

2. His most recent escape, the Pennington break-out, and the escape where he wore a guard's uniform occurred in three different states.

3. The 2009 escape didn't involve wire cutters.

4. Marco used a guard's uniform as a disguise 4 years after he broke out of Middle Fork prison.

5. The Alabama escape was 12 years before the one in Virginia.

6. Marco broke out of Lexington prison 12 years after his Middle Fork escape.

7. Of the two break-outs where Marco used a rope and a guard's uniform, one was at Calahatchee prison and the other was in 2005.

8. A rope made out of bedsheets was all Marco needed to break out of the prison in Colorado.

9. Marco wasn't in Montana in 2005, and he used neither wire cutters nor a tunnel for his Virginia escape.

	Prisons					States					Methods				
	Calahatchee	Lexington	Middle Fork	Pennington	Tulveride	Alabama	Colorado	Idaho	Montana	Virginia	Ladder	Rope	Tunnel	Uniform	Wire cutters
Years 2001															
2005															
2009															
2013															
2017															
Methods Ladder															
Rope															
Tunnel															
Uniform															
Wire cutters															
States Alabama															
Colorado															
Idaho															
Montana															
Virginia															

Years	Prisons	States	Methods
2001			
2005			
2009			
2013			
2017			

Answers on page 361.

For Stage and Screen

Every name listed below belongs to an actor who played Holmes in a Sherlock Holmes adaptation. Names can be found in a straight line horizontally, vertically, or diagonally. They may be read either forward or backward.

ALAN WHEATLEY

ARTHUR WONTNER

BASIL RATHBONE

BENEDICT CUMBER-BATCH

CHARLTON HESTON

CHRISTOPHER LEE

CLIVE BROOK

EILLE NORWOOD

GEOFFREY WHITEHEAD

HARRY ARTHUR SAINTS-BURY

IAN MCKELLEN

JEREMY BRETT

JOHN BARRYMORE

JONNY LEE MILLER

LEONARD NIMOY

MACK SENNETT

MAURICE COSTELLO

MICHAEL CAINE

NICHOLAS ROWE

NICOL WILLIAMSON

PATRICK MACNEE

ROBERT DOWNEY, JR.

ROBERT STEPHENS

WILLIAM GILLETTE

```
B E N E D I C T C U M B E R B A T C H Y H
H A R R Y A R T H U R S A I N T S B U R Y
E W O R S A L O H C I N C U Y I N A R K Y
O N C I M N C N P P T A E Q F M T U M R O
T L U S N E H P E T S T R E B O R B N Y K
E N I A C L E A H C I M T L V O M W Y R Y
C H A R L T O N H E S T O N M Q G P A W Y
D A E H E T I H W Y E R F F O E G B P S J
Y L R E D I D L B S V I E Y H W L A A A W
E A N I C O L W I L L I A M S O N S T R M
L N E T T E L L I G M A I L L I W I R T A
T R E L L I M E E L Y N N O J A X L I H C
A Y O M I N D R A N O E L X Z I O R C U K
E A Y R O B E R T D O W N E Y J R A K R S
H K O O R B E V I L C R J Q M X X T M W E
W N E L L E K C M N A I W N D R W H A O N
N J E R E M Y B R E T T N O W N J B C N N
A J O H N B A R R Y M O R E O G P O N T E
L C H R I S T O P H E R L E E D A N E N T
A Q Y W W Z X Q T Q F F W F B Y X E E E T
Q M A U R I C E C O S T E L L O A V V R K
```

Answers on page 361.

The Adventures of Sherlock Holmes Stories

Each word or phrase in all capitals in the Sherlock Holmes story titles below is contained within the group of letters. Words can be found horizontally, vertically, or diagonally. They may read either forward or backward.

SCANDAL in BOHEMIA

The RED-HEADED League

A Case of IDENTITY

The BOSCOMBE Valley MYSTERY

The Five ORANGE PIPS

The Man with the TWISTED LIP

The Adventure of the Blue CARBUNCLE

The Adventure of the SPECKLED Band

The Adventure of the ENGINEER's Thumb

The Adventure of the Noble BACHELOR

The Adventure of the BERYL CORONET

The Adventure of the COPPER BEECHES

```
O  B  D  S  P  I  P  E  G  N  A  R  O
S  E  H  C  E  E  B  R  E  P  P  O  C
P  R  E  L  J  J  T  W  V  D  E  A  L
I  Y  O  A  I  M  E  H  O  B  R  A  I
L  L  Y  L  Z  H  K  F  M  B  D  D  R
D  C  T  X  E  M  M  O  U  N  O  E  S
E  O  I  A  L  H  C  N  A  L  N  D  P
T  R  T  O  W  S  C  C  R  G  I  A  E
S  O  N  N  O  L  S  A  I  V  M  E  C
I  N  E  B  E  G  H  N  B  D  F  H  K
W  E  D  V  Y  R  E  T  S  Y  M  D  L
T  T  I  W  L  E  L  Y  L  H  F  E  E
I  S  W  Y  R  I  S  R  G  X  M  R  D
```

Answers on page 361.

For His Generation

Cryptograms are messages in substitution code. Break the code to read the message. For example, THE SMART CAT might become FVO QWGDF JGF if **F** is substituted for **T, V** for **H, O** for **E,** and so on.

VFX VZ GQX LVEG ZDLVJE PVBGBDUDCE

VZ QVCLXE MDLX ZBVL IDENC BDGQI-

VFX NF GQX ZVBGNXE. BDGQIVFX PC-

DUXS GQX SXGXMGNOX NF ZVJBGXXF

ZNCLE. XDBCNXB ZNCLE RXBX EXG NF

ONMGVBNDF GNLXE, RQNCX EVLX VZ

GQX CDGXB NFEGDCCDGNVFE RXBX

EXG NF GQX ZVBGNXE, RNGQ PCVGE

BXCDGXS GV GQX EXMVFS RVBCS RDB.

GQXBX RDE DCEV D BDSNV EXBNXE.

What Went Missing? (Part I)

The consulting detective visited the dressing room of the actress who had received threats. Examine the objects, then turn the page.

What Went Missing? (Part II)

Overnight, the actress got sick from poison and was rushed to the hospital! The consulting detective noted something missing from her dressing room and suspected it had contained the poison. From memory, can you work out what went missing?

Rental Agreements

Cryptograms are messages in substitution code. Break the code to read the message. For example, THE SMART CAT might become FVO QWGDF JGF if **F** is substituted for **T, V** for **H, O** for **E,** and so on. Bonus question: Who is described in the quote? Which story is the source of the quote?

EFN FEMW SHL CBJ KTJLN-KMFFJ KMHN TERHZ-
BZ HN HMM CFQJL PW NCJFEOL FK LTEOQMHJ
HEZ FKNBE QEZBLTJHPMB UCHJHUNBJL PQN
CBJ JBAHJYHPMB MFZOBJ LCFSBZ HE BUUBN-
JTUTNW HEZ TJJBOQMHJTNW TE CTL MTKB SC-
TUC AQLN CHRB LFJBMW NJTBZ CBJ GHNTBEUB.
CTL TEUJBZTPMB QENTZTEBLL, CTL HZZTUNT-
FE NF AQLTU HN LNJHEOB CFQJL, CTL FUUHLT-
FEHM JBRFMRBJ GJHUNTUB STNCTE ZFFJL, CTL
SBTJZ HEZ FKNBE AHMFZFJFQL LUTBENTKTU
BVGBJTABENL, HEZ NCB HNAFLGCBJB FK RT-
FMBEUB HEZ ZHEOBJ SCTUC CQEO HJFQEZ
CTA AHZB CTA NCB RBJW SFJLN NBEHEN TE
MFEZFE. FE NCB FNCBJ CHEZ, CTL GHWABENL
SBJB GJTEUBMW.

Fingerprint Match

Find the matching fingerprint(s). There may be more than one.

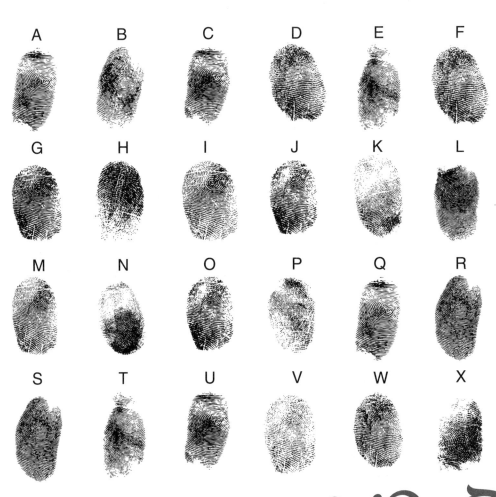

A B C D E F

G H I J K L

M N O P Q R

S T U V W X

Fingerprint Match

Find the matching fingerprint(s). There may be more than one.

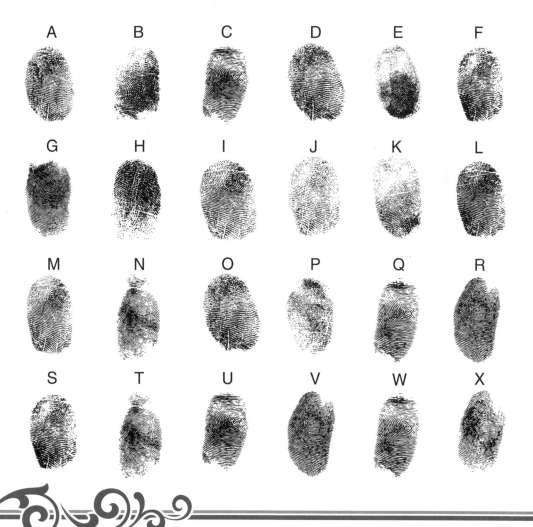

A B C D E F

G H I J K L

M N O P Q R

S T U V W X

Answers on page 362.

In Other Words

Cryptograms are messages in substitution code. Break the code to read the message. For example, THE SMART CAT might become FVO QWGDF JGF if **F** is substituted for **T, V** for **H, O** for **E,** and so on.

KWDGDWCK RGJ CWKLZJVGOK

VDPAOFZ KZPJZL, ZDVMCYLVP,

ROJLVQZ, KTYFGSW, PJWHLVP, YDF

PAYDFZKLVDZ.

Interception

You've intercepted a message that is meant to reveal a location for an upcoming meeting between two criminal masterminds. The only problem is, the message doesn't make sense. Can you figure out the right location?

WAUKESHA

SOUTH

ISLINGTON

GAULT

OMAN

DORIC

Answers on page 362.

A "Cork Shell Homes" Anagram

Below is a quotation from a Sherlock Holmes story. Fill in the blanks in each sentence with a word that is an anagram (rearrangement) of the capitalized word(s). Bonus: Name the Sherlock Holmes adventure from which this quotation is drawn.

Sherlock Holmes was a man who seldom took RICE EXES _____ for EXEC'S RISE _____ sake. Few men were capable of greater CUR MAULS _____ effort, and he was DOUBLY TUNED _____ one of the finest boxers of his TWIG HE _____ that I have ever seen; but he looked upon aimless bodily TIRE OXEN _____ as a waste of energy, and he seldom REST BRIDE _____ himself save when there was some professional object to be served. Then he was absolutely UNIT GRIN _____ and FAILING DEBATE _____. That he should have kept himself in TIN GRAIN _____ under such SCARCEST CUM-IN _____ is remarkable, but his diet was usually of the REPASTS _____, and his habits were simple to the verge of TEARY SUIT _____.

What Do You See? (Part I)

Study this picture of the crime scene for 1 minute, then turn the page.

What Do You See? (Part II)

(Do not read this until you have read the previous page!) Which image exactly matches the crime scene?

1

2

3

4

What Went Missing? (Part I)

At a client's house, the consulting detective saw many tools laid out. Study the objects, then turn the page.

What Went Missing? (Part II)

The following day, a guest was knocked over the head when he interrupted a theft in progress. Whatever was used as a weapon was taken away. The consulting detective sees that one object was missing from the previous day. From memory, can you work out what went missing?

Everybody and His Brother

Cryptograms are messages in substitution code. Break the code to read the message. For example, THE SMART CAT might become FVO QWGDF JGF if **F** is substituted for **T, V** for **H, O** for **E,** and so on.

PZLJH ZDHFILJADKH VKK AVPWKM LDK

BPEJNI MKLKZLFOK FY LDK 1962 EJOFK

IDKHVJZR DJVEKI PYM LDK MKPMVW

YKZRVPZK. FY 1970, VKK AVPWKM P

DJVEKI PCPFY–IDKHVJZR'I UHJLDKH

EWZHJBL, FY LDK EJOFK LDK AHFOPLK

VFBK JB IDKHVJZR DJVEKI. DK DPM

PVIJ AVPWKM IFH DKYHW UPIRKHOFV-

VK FY PY KPHVFKH BFVE PMPALKM

BHJE LDK DJNYM JB LDK UPIRKHOFV-

VKI.

Answers on page 362.

The Musgrave Ritual

Each word or phrase in all capitals in the Sherlock Holmes quotation below is contained within the group of letters. Words can be found horizontally, vertically, or diagonally. They may read either forward or backward.

Our CHAMBERS were always full of CHEMICALS and of criminal RELICS which had a way of wandering into unlikely positions, and of turning up in the BUTTER-DISH or in even less desirable places. But his PAPERS were my great CRUX. He had a horror of destroying DOCUMENTS, especially those which were connected with his past CASES, and yet it was only once in every year or two that he would MUSTER energy to DOCKET and arrange them; for, as I have mentioned somewhere in these incoherent MEMOIRS, the OUTBURSTS of passionate ENERGY when he performed the remarkable feats with which his name is associated were followed by reactions of LETHARGY during which he would lie about with his VIOLIN and his books, hardly moving save from the SOFA to the table. Thus month after month his papers ACCUMULATED, until every corner of the room was stacked with BUNDLES of manuscript which were on no account to be BURNED, and which could not be put away save by their OWNER.

```
D E B P Y A U A F O S N G T Z
X R I U R E T S U M W Y G B J
U N D O N A E A P F Z G P U J
R R I O H D O U T B U R S T S
C F S L C J L S R E P A P T S
B B E R O K I E G Y S H J E T
M W R M I I E S S G L T C R N
E L Z D X O V T E R A E H D E
R E L I C S M B K E C L N I M
R C U D O S U E W N I U N S U
E A I S C R V R M E M T Y H C
N S Y N N C H A M B E R S J O
W E Z E A X T N Q D H Q N E D
O S D H Z P G P Y O C A S T A
C D E T A L U M U C C A X H T
```

Answers on page 363.

The Suspect List

There's been a murder at the Forsyth Mansion! It happened sometime last evening during a fancy dinner party, and five guests who were present at the time are now considered possible suspects. Each has a different profession and is from a different town. None of the five men are the same age. Help the police sort out their investigation by matching each suspect to his age, profession, and home town.

1. Albert isn't the oldest of the five men.

2. The Flagstaff native is 3 years older than the suspect from Midvale (who isn't the dentist), and six years younger than the architect.

3. The engineer is older than Vincent.

4. Nicholas, who is from Billings, is 3 years older than Michael. Of the two of them, one is 26 years old and the other is the tennis pro.

5. The dentist isn't from Flagstaff.

6. Dennis lives in downtown San Pedro.

			Suspects				Professions					Towns				
		Albert	Dennis	Michael	Nicholas	Vincent	Architect	Dentist	Engineer	Lawyer	Tennis pro	Billings	Flagstaff	Midvale	San Pedro	Tulverton
Ages	23															
	26															
	29															
	32															
	35															
Towns	Billings															
	Flagstaff															
	Midvale															
	San Pedro															
	Tulverton															
Professions	Architect															
	Dentist															
	Engineer															
	Lawyer															
	Tennis pro															

Ages	Suspects	Professions	Towns
23			
26			
29			
32			
35			

143   *Answers on page 363.*

The Man with the Twisted Lip

Every word listed is contained within the group of letters. Words can be found in a straight line horizontally, vertically, or diagonally. They may be read either forward or backward.

BAKER STREET

BAR OF GOLD

BEGGAR

BRADSTREET

DIRTY SCOUNDREL

ELIAS

HUGH BOONE

ISA WHITNEY

KATE

NEVILLE ST CLAIR

OPIUM

SWANDAM LANE

```
Q Y Z L U B S M Y K O M W Y R
W G B G W E I A S W W Y Q B I
X R H E M G I O O A E O T R A
S A V K B G E D W N I Z T A L
L J J G W A K A T E F L E D C
W H D S E R J I S Q F A E S T
B U M E L J H W G V F I R T S
A G K X A W M T Y A X V T R E
R H E N A L M A D N A W S E L
O B D S O M S S J D P V R E L
F O I K T P A Y T M L S E T I
G O Q L Q T I V V B W Y K D V
O N M W X V U Q C N F A T E
L E O F K Y T T M M S H B J N
D I R T Y S C O U N D R E L D
```

Answers on page 363.

The Man with the Twisted Lip Letter

Each word or phrase in all capitals in the Sherlock Holmes quotation below is contained within the group of letters. Words can be found horizontally, vertically, or diagonally. They may read either forward or backward.

" 'DEAREST do not be FRIGHTENED. All will come well. There is a HUGE ERROR which it may take some little time to RECTIFY. Wait in PATIENCE.–NEVILLE.' Written in PENCIL upon the FLY-LEAF of a book, OCTAVO SIZE, no WATER-MARK. Hum! POSTED today in GRAVESEND by a man with a DIRTY THUMB. Ha! And the FLAP has been GUMMED, if I am not very much in error, by a person who had been CHEWING TOBACCO. And you have no doubt that it is your HUSBAND'S hand, MADAM?"

```
C G O M L N T S E R A E D I H
I R C W A T E R M A R K B I F
B A T D V Q M S Y A R J Y H H
E V A C W G V B I L S Q F U S
N E V I L L E P F L A P I G N
F S O A E J S D E I O M T E D
J E S C O C D R E N O J C E M
H N I T G P N S N M C A E R F
M D Z R O D A E E M M I R R A
E F E S B H B U I Q A U L O E
C B T A G G S Z F T D V G R L
D E K K W Y U W R S A O C R Y
D I R T Y T H U M B M P R Z L
O C C A B O T G N I W E H C F
F R I G H T E N E D O I Z T G
```

147

The Man with
the Twisted Lip Passage 1

Each word or phrase in all capitals in the Sherlock Holmes quotation below is contained within the group of letters. Words can be found horizontally, vertically, or diagonally. They may read either forward or backward.

NEVER IN MY LIFE have I seen SUCH A SIGHT. The man's face PEELED OFF under the SPONGE like the BARK FROM A TREE. Gone was the coarse BROWN TINT! Gone, too, was the horrid scar which had seamed it across, and the twisted lip which had given the REPULSIVE SNEER to the face! A TWITCH brought away the TANGLED red hair, and there, sitting up in his bed, was a pale, SAD-FACED, refined-looking man, BLACK-haired and SMOOTH-SKINNED, rubbing his eyes and staring about him with sleepy BEWILDERMENT. Then SUDDENLY realising the EXPOSURE, he broke into a SCREAM and THREW HIMSELF down with his face to the PILLOW.

```
R E P U L S I V E S N E E R E
F L E S M I H W E R H T I B E
I T F U G S A D F A C E D N R
O N I F T N I T N W O R B G T
C E L T O X Q Y U R O Q T H A
M M Y N I D E L G N A T G B M
P R M S E J E A U T E I Y A O
I E N U X E S L W S S L E B R
L D I D Y D G I E A E R R L F
L L R D I Z T N H E C F U A K
O I E E U C V C O S P E S C R
W W V N H Q U B Z P B K O K A
H E E L A S Y I F R S Q P M B
L B N Y M F S S Z H K C X Z S
N S M O O T H S K I N N E D J
```

Answers on page 363.

The Man with
the Twisted Lip Passage 2

Every all capital word listed is contained within the group of letters. Words can be found in a straight line horizontally, vertically, or diagonally. They may be read either forward or backward.

Through the GLOOM one could DIMLY catch a GLIMPSE of bodies

lying in strange FANTASTIC POSES, bowed shoulders, BENT KNEES,

heads THROWN back, and CHINS pointing UPWARD, with here and

there a dark, LACKLUSTRE eye turned upon the NEWCOMER. Out

of the BLACK SHADOWS there GLIMMERED little RED CIRCLES

of light, now bright, now faint, as the BURNING POISON waxed or

WANED in the BOWLS of the METAL PIPES. The most lay SILENT,

but some MUTTERED to themselves, and others talked together in a

STRANGE, low, MONOTONOUS voice, their CONVERSATION com-

ing in GUSHES, and then suddenly TAILING OFF into silence, each

MUMBLING out his own thoughts and paying LITTLE HEED to the

words of his NEIGHBOUR.

```
U G W W E G S W A W C T H R O W N P E
N N L S T R A N G E H T S Q I X P E H
L O R I C M L M T A I L I N G O F F U
N S Y L M O N O T O N O U S N L C S U
O I Y Z A P W X R V S H F F I X F Q J
I O X E R T S U L K C A L T L E C E X
T P L I T T L E H E E D U N B J G R S
A G D N E W C O M E R U E E M H K W D
S N C I C W J M H S X I P L U A O R U
R I D F Z H O S M E G J S I M D A B L
E N E I G O B B Q H V E E S A W O E W
V R R A L K L T B K P I P H P W X N A
N U E G D O W O A I F T S U L M C T N
O B T N I W U I P J T K Z S P Q G K E
C F T A M R D L J M C O W Z R X U N D
B G U Z L F A N T A S T I C P O S E S
D N M L Y T J G L I M M E R E D H E F
C F C G E J X B R E D C I R C L E S T
U C L M E E B B W V D U O T Z H S H O
```

Answers on page 364.

The Man with
the Twisted Lip Confession Pt. 1

Each word or phrase in all capitals in the Sherlock Holmes quotation below is contained within the group of letters. Words can be found horizontally, vertically, or diagonally. They may read either forward or backward.

You are the FIRST who have ever heard MY STORY. My FATHER was a SCHOOLMASTER in CHESTERFIELD, where I received an EXCELLENT EDUCATION. I TRAVELLED in my youth, TOOK TO THE STAGE, and finally became a REPORTER on an EVENING PAPER in LONDON. One day my EDITOR wished to have A SERIES OF ARTICLES upon BEGGING in the METROPOLIS, and I VOLUNTEERED to SUPPLY them. There was the point from which all my ADVENTURES started. It was only by trying begging as an AMATEUR that I could get the FACTS upon which to base my articles.

```
G R E C I B P Y Q S E I W D J E S S J
B P T J O D E O L Y Q K Y E F G E U P
B R U E T A M A X P D R F R I A L M B
L E D W I X M N S H P A B E D T C E X
B Y G E J A D V E N T U R E S S I T X
C W R G L N Z E E H L I S T U E T R S
H C E O I L O L E E I Q O N E H R O R
E T G L T N E R D Z G X H U I T A P F
S X X Q U S G V O N J P O L E O F O Y
T W H N R R Y S A K E U V O D T O L W
E Y P P O K L M M R G T G V Q K S I A
R K M T I D U Y G S T R S T P O E S K
F B I H Q N N R U H U A E R R O I G C
I D X I M G A O W I Q Y K T I T R Z K
E E R S C H O O L M A S T E R F E H C
L R E K D C X Q W C M O Y P J O S L Z
D B F F J I V H B W F G E F O P R M
N O I T A C U D E T N E L L E C X E P
Q M S A Q E V E N I N G P A P E R Q R
```

Answers on page 364.

The Man with the Twisted Lip Confession Pt. 2

Each word or phrase in all capitals in the Sherlock Holmes quotation below is contained within the group of letters. Words can be found horizontally, vertically, or diagonally. They may read either forward or backward.

When an ACTOR I had, OF COURSE, learned all the SECRETS of MAKING UP, and had been FAMOUS in the GREEN-ROOM for my skill. I TOOK ADVANTAGE now of my ATTAINMENTS. I painted my FACE, and to make myself as PITIABLE as POSSIBLE I made a GOOD SCAR and FIXED one side of my LIP IN A TWIST by the aid of a SMALL SLIP of FLESH-COLOURED plaster. Then with a RED HEAD OF HAIR, and an APPROPRIATE dress, I took my STATION in the BUSINESS part of the city, OSTENSIBLY as a MATCH-SELLER but really as a beggar. For SEVEN HOURS I plied my trade, and when I RETURNED home in the evening I found TO MY SURPRISE that I had received no less than 26s. 4d.

```
P  I  L  S  L  L  A  M  S  P  I  T  I  A  B  L  E
S  R  I  A  H  F  O  D  A  E  H  D  E  R  G  O  N
R  G  R  E  E  N  R  O  O  M  Y  B  W  H  Y  Y  X
U  T  S  I  W  T  A  N  I  P  I  L  T  Z  Y  L  E
O  O  Z  A  T  T  A  I  N  M  E  N  T  S  F  B  L
H  O  G  T  B  S  N  F  R  T  O  O  M  L  A  I  B
N  K  D  O  Q  U  I  O  A  E  F  L  E  N  M  S  I
E  A  E  W  O  X  S  X  I  C  T  S  U  A  O  N  S
V  D  F  A  E  D  A  I  O  T  H  U  K  J  U  E  S
E  V  G  D  N  C  S  U  N  C  A  I  R  R  S  T  O
S  A  O  L  T  D  R  C  O  E  N  T  Q  N  A  S  P
Y  N  V  O  E  S  N  L  A  G  S  M  S  J  E  O  I
F  T  R  Y  E  D  O  V  U  R  R  S  V  C  L  D  Z
H  A  W  C  N  U  A  P  P  R  O  P  R  I  A  T  E
V  G  C  G  R  N  Y  T  W  T  W  E  P  E  V  K  V
G  E  R  E  L  L  E  S  H  C  T  A  M  D  W  R  D
A  A  D  W  O  T  O  M  Y  S  U  R  P  R  I  S  E
```

Answers on page 364.

The Man with the Twisted Lip Confession Pt. 3

Every all capital word listed is contained within the group of letters. Words can be found in a straight line horizontally, vertically, or diagonally. They may be read either forward or backward.

I wrote my ARTICLES and thought LITTLE MORE of the MATTER until, SOME TIME LATER, I BACKED a bill for a FRIEND and had a WRIT served upon me for £25. I was at my WIT'S END where to get the MONEY, but a SUDDEN IDEA came to me. I begged a FORTNIGHT'S GRACE from the CREDITOR, asked for a HOLIDAY from my EMPLOYERS, and spent the time in BEGGING in the City under my DISGUISE. In TEN DAYS I had the money and had PAID THE DEBT.

```
S S O M E T I M E L A T E R G T A
J E M P L O Y E R S E C N I F Q E
A C F A V J I G W Y L J E Z J E W
Y A D I L O H C F E M N B M F Q B
P R N D Y I R R D N R B A X W S O
D G T T A N I Z Q O E Q C I Q U E
N S M H G E S L S M T Y K G T D R
E T E E N O U C D Y T T E N P D O
S H G D A G Z R Y X A W D I C E M
T G T E R A Q K O K M D Z G I N E
I I P B T W Z Y D T N Z N G K I L
W N F T I D I S G U I S E E D D T
K T V Z C E C A D M S D P B T E T
Y R J H L W C P A E W I E M Y A I
G O V I E R N C I V W E K R A G L
N F M N S I M A W Y U U Z X C I F
U A M A Y T D E B W Q I P A U X H
```

Answers on page 364.

The Man with
the Twisted Lip Confession Pt. 4

Each word or phrase in all capitals in the Sherlock Holmes quotation below is contained within the group of letters. Words can be found horizontally, vertically, or diagonally. They may read either forward or backward.

Well, you can IMAGINE how hard it was to SETTLE DOWN to ARDUOUS work at £2 a WEEK when I knew that I could earn as much in a day by SMEARING MY FACE with a little PAINT, laying my cap ON THE GROUND, and SITTING STILL. It was a LONG FIGHT between MY PRIDE and the MONEY, but the DOLLARS won at last, and I THREW UP reporting and sat DAY AFTER DAY in the CORNER which I had FIRST CHOSEN, inspiring PITY by my GHASTLY FACE and FILLING my pockets with COPPERS. Only one man knew my SECRET. He was the KEEPER of a LOW DEN in which I used to LODGE in SWANDAM LANE, where I could EVERY MORNING emerge as a SQUALID BEGGAR and in the evenings TRANSFORM myself into a well-dressed MAN ABOUT TOWN. This fellow was WELL PAID by me for his ROOMS, so that I knew that my secret was SAFE in his POSSESSION.

```
N W O D E L T T E S W S S P Q K Y T U K W
X K E E P E R W P B E L O N G F I G H T F
O F R E S O D H G C D I A P L L E W B R I
N G E G E R T H R E W U P K M L S I F U R
Q D N C H W O E O F E A R N O U H M G I S
O S R I V A T O B M D X Z B O P G R N U T
Z O O V L C S V M H L F R U Q C R O I X C
E L C B Y L X T O S D O D P R O S F N O H
S M R D I Q I X L R M R W J B W Q S R V O
N Y A D R E T F A Y A D U D Z O U N O M S
O S Q Y V Q E E S V F S D F E K A A M A E
I K R S E N I G A M I A D C F N L R Y N N
S B E B J S P D O E B D C D L F I T R A Z
S N L E N S V O Q H F V R E O A D E E B M
E F U U W K O L H R V A V Z L N B R V O Y
S I T T I N G S T I L L S Q K T E E E U P
S M E A R I N G M Y F A C E N M G Y K T R
O N T H E G R O U N D C J I O Z G S G T I
P Y H V D P F Z J J A X A N S R A L L O D
Y T I P C O P P E R S P E Q B S R S X W E
E N A L M A D N A W S Y H T O J B S O N Q
```

Answers on page 365.

The Man with the Twisted Lip Confession Pt. 5

Each word or phrase in all capitals in the Sherlock Holmes quotation below is contained within the group of letters. Words can be found horizontally, vertically, or diagonally. They may read either forward or backward.

Well, VERY SOON I found that I was saving CONSIDERABLE SUMS of money. I do not mean that any beggar in the STREETS OF LONDON could earn £700 a year—which is less than my AVERAGE TAKINGS—but I had EXCEPTIONAL advantages IN MY POWER of MAKING UP, and also in a FACILITY of REPARTEE, which IMPROVED by PRACTICE and made me quite a RECOGNISED CHARACTER in the City. All day a STREAM OF PENNIES, varied by SILVER, poured in upon me, and it was a VERY BAD DAY in which I FAILED to take £2.

As I grew RICHER I grew more AMBITIOUS, took a house in the country, and EVENTUALLY MARRIED, without anyone having a SUSPICION as to my REAL OCCUPATION. My DEAR WIFE knew that I had BUSINESS in the City. She LITTLE KNEW what.

```
E  I  N  R  S  T  R  E  A  M  O  F  P  E  N  N  I  E  S
W  T  L  O  L  W  U  E  S  V  E  R  Y  B  A  D  D  A  Y
S  K  J  Z  I  R  E  I  W  J  B  R  L  G  M  C  E  M  C
N  C  R  Z  X  T  L  N  Q  O  E  R  F  J  S  Y  I  B  O
O  X  I  A  B  V  A  B  K  N  P  A  X  G  U  J  R  I  N
D  C  C  N  E  U  Q  P  N  E  I  Y  N  U  E  M  R  T  S
N  P  H  R  T  F  S  B  U  L  L  I  M  B  N  A  A  I  I
O  R  E  Y  L  C  T  I  E  C  K  T  Q  N  L  K  M  O  D
L  A  R  Q  T  F  U  D  N  A  C  N  T  A  I  I  Y  U  E
F  C  J  U  G  I  C  R  T  E  S  O  N  I  U  N  L  S  R
O  T  S  M  D  L  L  E  E  X  S  O  L  E  L  G  L  K  A
S  I  D  G  E  E  G  I  Y  P  I  S  C  A  P  U  A  K  B
T  C  T  A  A  A  V  S  C  T  A  Y  I  Z  E  P  U  A  L
E  E  N  S  R  H  Q  O  P  A  E  R  G  Y  C  R  T  N  E
E  A  A  E  W  X  R  E  R  T  F  E  T  U  U  G  N  C  S
R  D  V  M  I  Q  C  D  K  P  Q  V  C  E  J  Y  E  F  U
T  A  X  F  F  X  C  H  Q  U  M  O  B  F  E  J  V  E  M
S  A  O  Z  E  S  U  S  P  I  C  I  O  N  R  G  E  X  S
R  E  T  C  A  R  A  H  C  D  E  S  I  N  G  O  C  E  R
```

Answers on page 365.

The Man with
the Twisted Lip Confession Pt. 6

Each word or phrase in all capitals in the Sherlock Holmes quotation below is contained within the group of letters. Words can be found horizontally, vertically, or diagonally. They may read either forward or backward.

LAST MONDAY I had FINISHED for the day and was DRESSING in my room above the OPIUM DEN when I LOOKED OUT of my WINDOW and saw, to my HORROR and ASTONISHMENT, that my WIFE was standing in the street, with her EYES FIXED FULL upon me. I gave a CRY OF SURPRISE, threw up my arms to COVER MY FACE, and, RUSHING to my CONFIDANT, the Lascar, ENTREATED him to PREVENT anyone from coming up to me. I heard her voice DOWNSTAIRS, but I knew that she could not ASCEND. Swiftly I threw off my CLOTHES, pulled on those of a beggar, and put on my PIGMENTS AND WIG.

```
E P F Z W M T H O A S C E N D L J
P I G M E N T S A N D W I G L G S
C R Y O F S U R P R I S E O A G R
X G B V V J I X C U W L P J S C I
P B E N T R E A T E D E R G T F A
X D K D H N G Z Q J F I E G M I T
A R F W O D N I W I Y K V J O N S
O E U F D M L S W V L Q E V N I N
P S A S T O N I S H M E N T D S W
I S U L H B S K K O B Q T Z A H O
U I J Z C I S V A R C J J D Y E D
M N V J L J N K H R U M V F E D M
D G H I O B Q G Y O G C U C S V J
E H S E T C O V E R M Y F A C E U
N P S K H C O N F I D A N T Y Z G
L O O K E D O U T K N P L B O Q A
M E Y E S F I X E D F U L L T C L
```

Answers on page 365.

The Man with
the Twisted Lip Confession Pt. 7

Each word or phrase in all capitals in the Sherlock Holmes quotation below is contained within the group of letters. Words can be found horizontally, vertically, or diagonally. They may read either forward or backward.

Even a wife's eyes could not PIERCE so COMPLETE a DISGUISE. But then it OCCURRED to me that there might be a SEARCH in the room, and that the clothes might BETRAY ME. I THREW OPEN the window, reopening by my VIOLENCE a SMALL CUT which I had INFLICTED upon myself in the bedroom THAT MORNING. Then I SEIZED MY COAT, which was WEIGHTED by the COPPERS which I had just TRANSFERRED to it from the LEATHER BAG in which I carried my TAKINGS. I HURLED it out of the window, and it DISAPPEARED into the THAMES. The other clothes would have FOLLOWED, but at THAT MOMENT there was a RUSH OF CONSTABLES up the stair, and a FEW MINUTES after I found, rather, I confess, TO MY RELIEF, that instead of being IDENTIFIED as MR. NEVILLE ST. CLAIR, I was ARRESTED as his MURDERER.

```
I  D  E  N  T  I  F  I  E  D  E  T  H  G  I  E  W  U  D
M  I  J  D  W  D  A  Z  C  D  I  S  G  U  I  S  E  U  G
Y  N  W  G  I  D  I  S  A  P  P  E  A  R  E  D  A  H  X
M  F  O  L  L  O  W  E  D  T  O  M  Y  R  E  L  I  E  F
R  P  N  T  V  W  Q  M  Q  O  B  S  E  A  R  C  H  G  T
N  R  U  S  H  O  F  C  O  N  S  T  A  B  L  E  S  N  T
E  L  G  G  Z  A  Z  D  E  T  C  I  L  F  N  I  T  I  A
V  S  U  A  Z  M  T  W  E  K  M  E  Z  K  F  D  H  N  K
I  R  A  B  F  E  W  M  I  N  U  T  E  S  F  L  R  R  I
L  E  D  R  T  O  Y  S  O  B  R  N  K  R  H  W  E  O  N
L  P  E  E  T  A  O  C  Y  M  D  E  Z  I  E  S  W  M  G
E  P  T  H  R  G  B  F  P  U  E  E  P  I  M  R  O  T  S
S  O  S  T  H  O  B  C  E  I  R  N  B  A  U  M  P  A  S
T  C  E  A  D  U  H  I  S  S  E  H  T  Y  M  E  E  H  Q
C  B  R  E  Y  Q  R  E  D  E  R  R  U  C  C  O  N  T  D
L  N  R  L  J  F  M  L  I  N  R  E  C  N  E  L  O  I  V
A  S  A  Y  L  A  I  O  E  D  T  E  T  E  L  P  M  O  C
I  R  H  G  H  C  R  E  W  D  C  S  M  A  L  L  C  U  T
R  W  M  T  T  C  K  D  E  R  R  E  F  S  N  A  R  T  O
```

Answers on page 365.

The Man with the Twisted Lip Confession Pt. 8

Each word or phrase in all capitals in the Sherlock Holmes quotation below is contained within the group of letters. Words can be found horizontally, vertically, or diagonally. They may read either forward or backward.

I do not know that there is ANYTHING ELSE for me to EXPLAIN. I was DETERMINED to PRESERVE my disguise AS LONG AS POSSIBLE, and hence my PREFERENCE for a DIRTY FACE. Knowing that my WIFE would be TERRIBLY ANXIOUS, I SLIPPED off my RING and CONFIDED it to the Lascar at a MOMENT when no CONSTABLE was watching me, TOGETHER with a HURRIED SCRAWL, telling her that she had NO CAUSE TO FEAR.

```
E  R  D  I  R  T  Y  F  A  C  E  V  W  A  L  C  P
L  A  V  H  C  B  Y  D  O  G  T  U  T  I  H  E  R
B  E  W  U  W  T  U  N  E  A  Y  M  J  U  F  N  E
I  F  L  R  W  D  F  P  Y  N  U  E  J  Y  L  E  S
S  O  L  R  Q  I  E  P  L  Y  I  R  C  H  Q  F  E
S  T  Z  I  D  H  K  P  L  T  G  M  X  H  R  O  R
O  E  V  E  G  Q  J  V  P  H  C  D  R  I  N  G  V
P  S  D  D  F  P  Z  E  E  I  S  H  R  E  H  T  E
S  U  R  S  U  R  P  S  N  N  L  A  U  N  T  Z  A
A  A  E  C  U  E  I  D  P  G  K  S  A  I  I  E  M
G  C  H  R  Y  F  E  H  W  E  B  V  Z  A  A  P  D
N  O  T  A  J  E  D  T  B  L  M  N  E  L  Z  X  E
O  N  E  W  Y  R  D  X  O  S  J  O  W  P  K  L  D
L  T  G  L  I  E  M  Y  N  E  A  N  M  X  I  H  C
S  U  O  I  X  N  A  Y  L  B  I  R  R  E  T  H  O
A  C  T  P  S  C  M  Z  F  S  K  E  D  M  N  R  Q
N  O  H  C  B  E  C  O  N  S  T  A  B  L  E  T  X
```

167

Answers on page 366.

Another Resident of Baker Street

Cryptograms are messages in substitution code. Break the code to read the message. For example, THE SMART CAT might become FVO QWGDF JGF if **F** is substituted for **T**, **V** for **H**, **O** for **E**, and so on.

XF HMN HNPNLXEXYF EMYO MYIEN, HMN HX-

HPN WMBDBWHND, RDNRYDU MYIEN, OBE

JBDHPU XFEJXDNZ QU BFZ MBE TBFU WMBD-

BWHNDXEHXWE XF WYTTYF OXHM HMN GX-

WHXYFBP ZNHNWHXLN NLNF HMYIRM HMN

TUEHNDXNE MN EYPLNZ ONDN TNZXWBP

XFEHNBZ YG WDXTXFBP. EMYDN, HMN EMYO'E

WDNBHYD, OBE B QXR GBF. MYIEN, PXKN MXE

JDNZNWNEEYD, OBE XDBEWXQPN, MBZ B WYT-

JBFXYF (CBTNE OXPEYF XFEHNBZ YG CYMF

OBHEYF), BFZ NLNF PXLNZ YF QBKND EHD-

NNH! HMN FBTNE MYIEN, XF GBWH, EYIFZE

PXKN "MYTNE," B MYTYFUT YG HMN ZNHNWHX-

LN'E FBTN.

What Went Missing? (Part I)

The consulting detective met his client on Thursday, and was told that a family heirloom, a diamond, was hidden somewhere in the room because the client had received demands for it. This was the room in which they met. Examine the room, then turn the page.

What Went Missing? (Part II)

The next day, the consulting detective was called back because his client had disappeared. The consulting detective noted that something else had gone missing. From memory, can you work out what went missing?

Duality

Cryptograms are messages in substitution code. Break the code to read the message. For example, THE SMART CAT might become FVO QWGDF JGF if **F** is substituted for **T, V** for **H, O** for **E,** and so on.

XQOT QDJMHI EQPK BYQTKN EMYXKI, QON

XQOT EQPK BYQTKN RQJIMO–ZLJ ZHGJGIE QD-

JMH BQJHGDA XQDOKK RQI MOK MU JEK UKR

JM BYQT ZMJE HMYKI NLHGOV Q YMOV DQH-

KKH! EK BYQTKN JEK DEQHQDJKH MU RQJIMO

MBBMIGJK HMVKH XMMHK QON DEHGIJM-

BEKH YKK. QON JM DQB GJ MUU, GO 1984, EK

BYQTKN Q DEQHQDJKH MO JEK JKYKPGIGMO

IEMR XQVOLX B.G. REM EQN Q NKYLIGMO JEQJ

EK RQI IEKHYMDA EMYXKI.

Answers on page 366.

The Red-Headed League Characters

Every word listed is contained within the group of letters. Words can be found in a straight line horizontally, vertically, or diagonally. They may be read either forward or backward.

ARCHIE

DR. JOHN WATSON

DUNCAN ROSS

JABEZ WILSON

JOHN CLAY

MR. MERRYWEATHER

PETER JONES

SHERLOCK HOLMES

VINCENT SPAULDING

WILLIAM MORRIS

```
H T E E N Q Y N W B E A Y H S G G
F S I R R O M M A I L L I W H D N
S L D D F N S G Y L S I L R R R I
R E U Y F C T L D R C U V I G N D
E L N Z M B G D I A E R C E V V L
H D N O C L K H G W E G G L K X U
T F O K J W V B B Y Z I Y Z N D A
A S S W G R U T E P H E H L L U P
E F T E A S E M E H S J B C O N S
W Y A Y K C M T P I O Z O A R C T
Y F W Q Z B P G E H K K U G J A N
R G N E Y F Y X N P O Y N T S N E
R S H E R L O C K H O L M E S R C
E T O Z E I L U V W F I M C M O N
M J J R N A U I E I H U W Y Y S I
R L R X Y D L L U W J J V X Q S V
M U D L L W Z E Q G P S H V M J H
```

173   Answers on page 366.

Each word or phrase in all capitals in the Sherlock Holmes quotation below is contained within the group of letters. Words can be found horizontally, vertically, or diagonally. They may read either forward or backward.

"AS A RULE," said Holmes, "the MORE BIZARRE a thing is the LESS MYSTERIOUS it PROVES to be. It is your commonplace, FEATURE-LESS crimes which are really PUZZLING, just as a COMMONPLACE face is the MOST DIFFICULT to IDENTIFY. But I must be PROMPT over this MATTER."

```
Z  L  H  R  R  V  U  Y  T  Y  Z  L  R  K  W
R  G  N  I  L  Z  Z  U  P  J  D  G  P  T  C
B  T  W  V  R  F  E  L  U  R  A  S  A  A  R
E  R  R  A  Z  I  B  E  R  O  M  E  C  Y  T
F  E  A  T  U  R  E  L  E  S  S  Y  O  P  R
S  A  U  X  E  H  X  V  E  A  F  Y  M  U  F
I  Y  T  O  P  U  I  G  X  I  W  O  M  J  T
O  L  E  S  S  M  Y  S  T  E  R  I  O  U  S
S  Z  M  G  L  G  R  N  Z  P  C  I  N  A  Q
M  E  E  A  Y  S  E  M  O  U  X  H  P  X  Y
L  Z  V  Z  T  D  M  H  F  I  A  H  L  O  D
U  U  M  O  I  T  A  B  R  J  L  L  A  Z  D
M  K  Z  W  R  C  E  A  X  U  H  I  C  U  Z
Y  C  D  N  O  P  I  R  P  W  W  U  E  T  C
M  O  S  T  D  I  F  F  I  C  U  L  T  C  B
```

Answers on page 367.

The Red-Headed League Passage 2

Each word or phrase in all capitals in the Sherlock Holmes quotation below is contained within the group of letters. Words can be found horizontally, vertically, or diagonally. They may read either forward or backward.

I TRUST that I am not MORE DENSE than my NEIGHBOURS, but I was always OPPRESSED with a SENSE of my own STUPIDITY in my DEALINGS with Sherlock Holmes. Here I had HEARD what he had heard, I had seen what he had SEEN, and yet from his WORDS it was EVIDENT that he saw clearly not only what had HAPPENED but what was ABOUT to happen, while to me the whole BUSINESS was still CONFUSED and GROTESQUE.

```
N E I G H B O U R S X K D
L O P P R E S S E D T C E
B J P X D O K Y J R L C A
E U T R U S T T T O H O L
E D S M E E H E K W T N I
V E T I O S P E S V Z F N
I N U X N R N W A Q F U G
D E P D D E E T R U S S
E P I T E O S D S I D E N
N P D K U Q G S E O E D O
T A I Z U O S C N N V J U
U H T W A V B V T M S L G
A V Y V I H N A Z B E E Y
```

Answers on page 367.

The Red-Headed League Passage 3

Every all capital word listed is contained within the group of letters. Words can be found in a straight line horizontally, vertically, or diagonally. They may be read either forward or backward.

"You will REMEMBER that I REMARKED the OTHER DAY, just before we went into the VERY SIMPLE problem presented by MISS MARY SUTHERLAND, that for STRANGE effects and EXTRAORDINARY combinations we must go to LIFE ITSELF, which is always far more DARING than any EFFORT of the IMAGINATION."

"A PROPOSITION which I took the LIBERTY of DOUBTING."

"You did, DOCTOR, but none the less you must COME ROUND to my view, for OTHERWISE I shall keep on piling FACT UPON FACT on you until your reason BREAKS DOWN under them and ACKNOWLEDG-ES me to be right.

```
H R E M E M B E R O T H E R W I S E A
F A C T U P O N F A C T Y C P I T T A
M K D G N I R A D E C B E G M T V P W
T Z G P R X F M X D R E M A R K E D A
R A E P N N A Y O V G J G A E U W B L
Z Y X H P B M C T V K I D G L C C B I
U V T P C R T S G N N M Y N P I S I F
S E R L I O O U E A T J W T M T E R E
O C A H R Z X P T U L O G L I S G R I
T N O T K J J I O Y D Y Y V S C D Q T
H H R O J H O O K S O Q A U Y I E I S
E U D F J N S N K G I B L R R Y L H E
R E I Q P F M A O K S T F N E H W D L
D H N L Q Q E Y T R E B I L V M O O F
A N A R W R E G N A R T S O G W N X Q
Y T R D B R R N E F F O R T N C K K M
W C Y X D N U O R E M O C K X W C E C
U M I S S M A R Y S U T H E R L A N D
H O Q S M Z U B K O P D O U B T I N G
```

Answers on page 367.

Each word or phrase in all capitals in the Sherlock Holmes quotation below is contained within the group of letters. Words can be found horizontally, vertically, or diagonally. They may read either forward or backward.

As he GLANCED down the ADVERTISEMENT COLUMN, with his head THRUST FORWARD and the paper FLATTENED out upon his KNEE, I took a GOOD LOOK at the man and ENDEAVOURED, after the FASHION of my COMPANION, to read the INDICATIONS which might be presented by his dress or APPEARANCE.

I did not gain very much, however, by my INSPECTION. Our VISITOR bore EVERY MARK of being an AVERAGE commonplace BRITISH TRADESMAN, obese, POMPOUS, and SLOW.

```
N B S I G A H Y E T A S O T F D Q X C
A J B D R A W R O F T S U R H T G O T
M A O Z W D T O F A K N E E S H M C T
S N O I T A C I D N I V Z G E P R M F
E E V F B E C A L Z I C A B A S L O W
D R B I K O N D P K R V V N B A U B J
A R K N Q J U D A J E V I S I T O R D
R S R S J D P Z E R L O E B C F U K M
T L A P H G R D A A N D W N Q A C P F
H I M E L Q Q G S P V R Q F C S Z G P
S F Y C A F E I Y N Y O R F D H P L C
I F R T K O O L D O O G U P L I O A S
T L E I J O C E C Z L H Y R C O M N Z
I N V O L Q Y V A T J H W A E N P C M
R V E N U W U H B L M M Q K X D O E V
B P H Q V V D S P G F S R P G P U D W
K C S S X A P P E A R A N C E F S V H
T A V Z T E X L O F L A T T E N E D Q
A D V E R T I S E M E N T C O L U M N
```

181

Answers on page 367.

The Red-Headed League Passage 5

Each word or phrase in all capitals in the Sherlock Holmes quotation below is contained within the group of letters. Words can be found horizontally, vertically, or diagonally. They may read either forward or backward.

"LET ME SEE," said Holmes, STANDING at the CORNER and glancing ALONG THE LINE, "I should like just to remember the ORDER of the houses here. It is a HOBBY of mine to have an EXACT KNOWLEDGE of LONDON. There is MORTIMER'S, the TOBACCONIST, the little NEWSPAPER SHOP, the COBURG BRANCH of the City and SUBURBAN Bank, the VEGETARIAN Restaurant, and MCFARLANE'S carriage-building DEPOT.

```
L T U N T M Z A R E N R O C S
N H X Z N A I R A T E G E V U
E Z O T B I B L U D U T F Q B
W H L B Y Z E A R D E P O T U
S P G P B L K O C D X P O J R
P A E E P Y E M L C Q N C X B
A E N I L E H T G N O L A O A
P B H D O J Y X M I E N O R N
E O A M O R T I M E R S I M K
R Z V S B N H N J R S J E S V
S L O J O T B S X G N E A A T
H O U D M C F A R L A N E S L
O B N C O B U R G B R A N C H
P O E F S M S T A N D I N G R
L E X A C T K N O W L E D G E
```

Answers on page 368.

The Red-Headed League Passage 6

Each word or phrase in all capitals in the Sherlock Holmes quotation below is contained within the group of letters. Words can be found horizontally, vertically, or diagonally. They may read either forward or backward.

Sherlock Holmes' QUICK EYE took in my OCCUPATION, and he SHOOK his head WITH A SMILE as he noticed my QUESTIONING glances. "Beyond the OBVIOUS FACTS that he has at some time done MANUAL LABOUR, that he takes SNUFF, that he is a FREEMASON, that he has been in CHINA, and that he has done a CONSIDERABLE amount of WRITING lately, I can deduce NOTHING ELSE."

```
W C O N S I D E R A B L E
R M A N U A L L A B O U R
I Q N L O X Z Y J C P G E
T N A O S S I S C Y K B L
I B W N T P A U H M X V I
N A U N Z H P M F O A F M
G F N J K A I K E Y O Y S
F E G I T S V N W E B K A
O E A I H P J L G W R Q H
B Q O S N C J F T E V F T
B N Q U I C K E Y E L S I
O B V I O U S F A C T S W
Q U E S T I O N I N G Z E
```

Answers on page 368.

The Red-Headed League
Newspaper Listing

Each word or phrase in all capitals in the Sherlock Holmes quotation below is contained within the group of letters. Words can be found horizontally, vertically, or diagonally. They may read either forward or backward.

"To The Red-Headed League: ON ACCOUNT of the BEQUEST of the late EZEKIAH Hopkins, of LEBANON, Pennsylvania, U. S. A., there is now another VACANCY open which ENTITLES a MEMBER of the League to a SALARY of £4 a week for PURELY NOMINAL services. All red-headed men who are sound in BODY AND MIND and above the age of TWENTY-ONE YEARS, are ELIGIBLE. Apply in person on MONDAY, at ELEVEN O'CLOCK, to DUNCAN ROSS, at the offices of the League, 7 Pope's Court, FLEET STREET."

```
M P L A N I M O N Y L E R U P
G T J H F F L X R M I B M T R
W D J A N O N A B E L O K W Y
E L B I G I L E A O F D C E X
A N J S Y A S X C Z D Y O N A
C W X S S W R G V T Z A L T S
B A Y O B R F V A C A N C Y B
Q R O R B E Q U E S T D O O S
Y S A N E B T E V J H M N N E
X A X A O M I V H O A I E E L
E W D C J E J Y T Y I N V Y T
O A A N D M A H J P K D E E I
S T N U O C C A N O E H L A T
S H M D W M B O I F Z Y E R N
B Y F L E E T S T R E E T S E
```

Answers on page 368.

Stop, Thief!

Cryptograms are messages in substitution code. Break the code to read the message. For example, THE SMART CAT might become FVO QWGDF JGF if **F** is substituted for **T**, **V** for **H**, **O** for **E**, and so on.

CPC WYH MVYL FGKF FGR QKTYHB CRFRN-

FPJR UYBF GPB QPEBF NKBR? GPB QPEBF

NKBR YV QPUT, FGKF PB. PV 1900, K BGYEF

BPURVF QPUT NKUURC, "BGREUYNM GYUTRB

AKQQURC," LKB NERKFRC. PV FGR QPUT, KV

PVFEHCRE ERDRKFRCUW NYTRB PVFY QEKTR

KVC BFRKUB QEYT FGR BURHFG. KB DEYTP-

BRC PV FGR FPFUR, FGR AHEZUKE ZRFB KLKW

HVBNKFGRC. YQ NYHEBR, FGR QPUT YVUW

EHVB FGPEFW BRNYVCB, BY DREGKDB OHBF-

PNR LYHUC GKJR DERJKPURC PQ FGR QPUTB-

FEPD GKC NYVFPVHRC.

What Do You See (Part I)

Study this picture of the crime scene for 1 minute, then turn the page.

What Do You See? (Part II)

(Do not read this until you have read the previous page!) Which image exactly matches the crime scene?

1

2

3

4

Answers on page 368.

For His Generation

Cryptograms are messages in substitution code. Break the code to read the message. For example, THE SMART CAT might become FVO QWGDF JGF if **F** is substituted for **T, V** for **H, O** for **E,** and so on.

VITIDN LTIRR AEMNIJ RXI SEIQRX WC

M EBCY-TQCCWCY RIEIPWSWBC SITWIS

ATBJQKIJ LN YTMCMJM RIEIPWSWBC

WC RXI IWYXRWIS MCJ CWCIRWIS. ZB-

TRN-RGB BZ MTRXQT KBCMC JBNEI'S

SRBTWIS GITI MJMARIJ ZBT RXI SIT-

WIS, MCJ RXI SITWIS XMJ M TIAQRM-

RWBC ZBT LIWCY ZMWRXZQE RB RXI

LBBFS. LTIRR XMJ MKRQMEEN AEMNIJ

GMRSBC WC 1980, MKTBSS ZTBD KXM-

TERBC XISRBC'S XBEDIS.

Answers on page 369.

The Adventure of the Copper Beeches

Every word listed is contained within the group of letters. Words can be found in a straight line horizontally, vertically, or diagonally. They may be read either forward or backward.

ADVANCE	JEPHRO
BLACK SWAN	MASTIFF
CARLO	MISS STOPER
CHESTNUT	MR FOWLER
COUNTRYSIDE	PHILADELPHIA
ELECTRIC BLUE	RUCASTLE
GOVERNESS	TOLLERS
HAIRCUT	VIOLET HUNTER
HAMPSHIRE	WESTAWAY
HIDDEN WING	WINCHESTER

```
J A C O U N T R Y S I D E V N E U
G G O V E R N E S S L K U G A J Y
H D S Q O V S L F F I T S A M N N
X V L X U Z C W D L O R C K G L S
B I P E O A U O H X F K E T N R E
R O O Q R Z E F W S A C D U I T L
M L H L V I F R Y W N V E N W N T
I E O M N I H M V A G A K T N A S
S T F F P S S V Y L Z U S E W A
S H O B P A G D P X D C W E D S C
S U G E L D A Y T M R H E H D K U
T N J E P H R O D I A J S C I C R
O T O L L E R S A L G H T K H A U
P E R E T S E H C N I W A F R L G
E R A F B G I Z A J F M W Y B B Q
R P H I L A D E L P H I A I Q P T
E L E C T R I C B L U E Y O J P P
```

193

Answers on page 369.

Cryptograms are messages in substitution code. Break the code to read the message. For example, THE SMART CAT might become FVO QWGDF JGF if **F** is substituted for **T, V** for **H, O** for **E,** and so on.

EGVKA'H HLGFBAH SAFA HAFBUKBWAE BP U

XUZUWBPA IUKKAE LQA HLFUPE, UPE UIIGX-

CUPBAE OV BKKNHLFULBGPH IFAULAE OV HBE-

PAV CUZAL. LQA BEAU LQUL QGKXAH SGFA U

EAAFHLUKMAF IUC UPE UP BPRAFPAHH IUCA

IGXAH PGL EBFAILKV JFGX EGVKA ONL JFGX

CUZAL'H BKKNHLFULBGPH. CUZAL QUE LSG

OFGLQAFH, OGLQ BKKNHLFULGFH; OV GPA

UIIGNPL, OFGLQAF SUKLAF SUH GFBZBPUKKV

BPLAPEAE LG EG LQA JBFHL BKKNHLFULBGPH,

ONL LQA CNOKBHQAFH HAPL LQA KALLAF LG

HBEPAV BPHLAUE.

What Do You See? (Part I)

Study this picture of the crime scene for 1 minute, then turn the page.

What Do You See? (Part II)

(Do not read this until you have read the previous page!) Which image exactly matches the crime scene?

1

2

3

4

What Changed? (Part I)

The consulting detective's friends like to challenge him. They lined up the series of bottles seen below. Examine the objects, then turn the page.

What Changed? (Part II)

The detective's friends made one change to the objects and showed them to him again. From memory, can you say what changed?

An Enduring Trait

Cryptograms are messages in substitution code. Break the code to read the message. For example, THE SMART CAT might become FVO QWGDF JGF if **F** is substituted for **T,** V for **H,** O for **E,** and so on.

NEP ZPNPVNORP'L LOFAJNQKP VJBJG-

JLE DODP TJL DCDQBJKOYPZ GW TOB-

BOJM FOBBPNNP, TEC DBJWPZ ECBMPL

CA LNJFP OA NEP BJNP 1800L JAZ PJK-

BW 1900L. LOZAPW DJFPN'L OBBQLNK-

JNOCAL LECTPZ NEP LBPQNE TONE J

LNKJOFEN DODP, GQN FOBBPNNP QLPZ

J VQKRW VJBJGJLE DODP, J ZPNJOB

NEJN BJLNPZ OA NEP ZPVJZPL NEJN

HCBBCTPZ.

The Adventure of
the Resident Patient

Each word or phrase in all capitals in the Sherlock Holmes quotation below is contained within the group of letters. Words can be found horizontally, vertically, or diagonally. They may read either forward or backward.

In glancing over the somewhat INCOHERENT series of Memoirs with which I have ENDEAVORED to ILLUSTRATE a few of the mental PECULIARITIES of my friend Mr. Sherlock Holmes, I have been struck by the difficulty which I have experienced in picking out EXAMPLES which shall in every way answer my PURPOSE. For in those cases in which Holmes has performed some TOUR DE FORCE of analytical REASONING, and has demonstrated the VALUE of his peculiar methods of INVESTIGATION, the facts themselves have often been so SLIGHT or so COMMONPLACE that I could not feel JUSTIFIED in laying them before the PUBLIC. On the other hand, it has frequently happened that he has been concerned in some RESEARCH where the facts have been of the most remarkable and DRAMATIC character, but where the share which he has himself taken in determining their causes has been less PRONOUNCED than I, as his BIOGRAPHER, could wish. The small matter which I have CHRONICLED under the heading of "A Study in Scarlet," and that other later one connected with the loss

of the Gloria Scott, may serve as examples of this SCYLLA and CHA-RYBDIS which are forever threatening the HISTORIAN.

```
B Z S E L P M A X E E E L X K W N
V I P U U E C A L P N O M M O C K
R L S L X N L I N C O H E R E N T
X L R A J U S T I F I E D T Y F B
E U E V K M D L K H K A J O T F I
M S A P N J B E L Z S M E U H P O
S T S P Q U A L L Y C S E R G U G
Y R O A P N V Q F C F P U D I R R
U A N E U J G S F O I X O E L P A
R T I C I T A M A R D N G F S O P
E E N L I T G Q L U N I O O L S H
S A G M M D E C N U O N O R P E E
E N D E A V O R E D P O T C H O R
A S I D B Y R A H C U M Q E U C P
R S J Q N O I T A G I T S E V N I
C N A I R O T S I H D C C T R K B
H P E C U L I A R I T I E S U Y O
```

Answers on page 370.

Cryptograms are messages in substitution code. Break the code to read the message. For example, THE SMART CAT might become FVO QWGDF JGF if **F** is substituted for **T, V** for **H, O** for **E,** and so on.

NMZ JDYZK LNKZZN LNFG FE NMZ AFE-

VFE OEVZKHKFOEV MDL NRAZL NMDN

LMFS NMZ LRAMFOZNNZ FC NMZ BFLN

CDBFOL (RC CRPNRFEDA) KZLRVZEN

FC NMDN LNKZZN. EZDKJW RL D BOL-

ZOB VZQFNZV NF NMZ BDE DEV MRL

SFKY.

What Went Missing? (Part I)

The consulting detective visited the study of a writer who had received mysterious notes. Examine the objects on the writer's desk, then turn the page.

What Went Missing? (Part II)

The next day, the writer was attacked! The butler rushed in to see a mysterious assailant who fled, and the butler got the writer to the hopsital. From the wounds, the writer was stabbed by something sharp, but the assailant fled with the weapon. The consulting detective visited the scene and noted the absence of an object that was the likely weapon. From memory, can you work out what went missing?

What Went Missing? (Part I)

The consulting detective met his client on Thursday, and was told that some old family documents were hidden somewhere in the room. This was the room in which they met. Examine the room, then turn the page.

What Went Missing? (Part II)

On Friday, the consulting detective was called back because his client had disappeared. The consulting detective noted that something else had gone missing. From memory, can you work out what went missing?

Murder and Stolen Gems

The letters in ONYX can be found in boxes 6, 13, 19 and 22, but not necessarily in that order. Similarly, the letters in all the other valuables can be found in the boxes indicated. Your task is to insert all the letters of the alphabet into the boxes. If you do this correctly, the shaded cells will reveal two gem stones.

AQUAMARINE: 2, 4, 6, 7, 10, 11, 14, 25

BERYL: 4, 10, 12, 13, 17

CORAL: 2, 5, 10, 17, 22

EMERALD: 2, 3, 4, 10, 14, 17

FIRE OPAL: 2, 4, 10, 17, 20, 22, 23, 25

GARNET: 2, 4, 6, 10, 16, 18

IVORY: 9, 10, 13, 22, 25

JASPER: 1, 2, 4, 10, 21, 23

JEWELS: 1, 4, 17, 21, 26

KUNZITE: 4, 6, 8, 11, 15, 16, 25

ONYX: 6, 13, 19, 22

SAPPHIRE: 2, 4, 10, 21, 23, 24, 25

TOPAZ: 2, 15, 16, 22, 23

1	2	3	4	5	6	7	8	9	10	11	12	13

14	15	16	17	18	19	20	21	22	23	24	25	26

 Answers on page 370.

The Cat Burglar

Maurice St. Clair is considered by many to be the most successful cat burglar of the 20th century. As a local crime reporter, you've been given an assignment to write a story about six of his most daring heists spanning more than 30 years. Using only the clues below, match each of these thefts to the correct month, year, and location, and determine what was stolen in each.

1. The 1991 theft (which wasn't in Seattle) was either the one that happened on July 4th or the one involving the collection of rare blue diamonds.

2. The cash heist, the one in 1998, and the one that took place on April 13th were three different events.

3. Maurice's infamous "Halloween heist" (so-called because it happened on October 31st) didn't involve either diamonds or rubies.

4. Of the cash theft and the Vancouver heist, one happened in July and the other occurred in 1984.

5. The Berlin burglary happened 7 years after the Halloween heist.

6. Of Maurice's 1991 burglary and the one that happened in Paris, one involved blue diamonds and the other occurred on June 15th.

7. The September theft happened sometime after Maurice's infamous London heist.

8. The Seattle heist (which didn't happen in the 1980s) didn't take place in July.

9. The Halloween heist happened 7 years before Maurice's September 10th theft (which involved a large number of pure gold bars).

10. The emerald theft happened sometime before the June 15th heist.

11. The July 4th heist occurred 14 years after the sapphire burglary.

	Cities						Items						Months					
	Antwerp	Berlin	London	Paris	Seattle	Vancouver	Cash	Diamonds	Emeralds	Gold bars	Rubies	Sapphires	April	May	June	July	October	September
1963																		
1970																		
1977																		
1984																		
1991																		
1998																		
April																		
May																		
June																		
July																		
October																		
September																		
Cash																		
Diamonds																		
Emeralds																		
Gold bars																		
Rubies																		
Sapphires																		

Years	Cities	Items	Months
1963			
1970			
1977			
1984			
1991			
1998			

Answers on page 370.

Marked Bills

The local police have been tracking a series of marked bills that were stolen during a recent string of bank robberies, in an effort to capture the perpetrators. So far, five such bills have been located. Each was used in a different place and on a different day, and each bill was of a different denomination (such as a $10 or a $20). Using only the clues below, match each marked bill to the date and location in which it was spent, and determine the serial number and denomination of each one.

1. C-918303 was used 8 days after the bill that popped up in Midvale.

2. The $100 bill wasn't spent on April 13th.

3. P-101445 was either the $20 bill or the one used on April 5.

4. The $5 bill with the serial number B-492841 was used 4 days after F-667280, but not in Finsberg.

5. The Midvale bill was used 4 days after G-718428 was passed somewhere in Torbin.

6. The marked $20 bill was spent 4 days after the one in Nettleton.

7. Neither the $10 bill nor the $100 bill was used on April 1st.

	Serials					Locations					Denominations				
	B-492841	C-918303	F-667280	G-718428	P-101445	Finsberg	Midvale	Nettleton	Torbin	Uteville	$5	$10	$20	$50	$100
Dates April 1															
April 5															
April 9															
April 13															
April 17															
Denominations $5										
$10										
$20										
$50										
$100										
Locations Finsberg					
Midvale					
Nettleton					
Torbin					
Uteville					

Dates	Serials	Locations	Denominations
April 1			
April 5			
April 9			
April 13			
April 17			

211

Answers on page 370.

Rare Wines

Georgina Guernsey's prized wine cellar was broken into last night, and five of her most rare bottles were stolen! She's absolutely beside herself…especially since she was planning on having her annual Spring garden party this weekend. Help the police figure out what's missing by matching each missing bottle of wine to its type, vintage year, and country of origin.

1. The Friambliss was bottled 8 years before the French wine.

2. The syrah, the Friambliss, and the Spanish wine were bottled in three different years.

3. The Weimerund isn't a merlot, and it wasn't bottled in 1958.

4. Of the Ece Suss and the 1970 bottle, one is from Greece and the other is a merlot.

5. The 1958 bottle is either the pinot gris or the Spanish wine.

6. Ania Branco wasn't ever made in France.

7. The Italian wine was bottled 4 years before the Spanish one, which wasn't the chardonnay.

8. Of the merlot and the pinot gris, one was from France and the other was a 1962 vintage.

9. The 1966 wine wasn't a syrah.

	Wines					Types					Countries				
	Ania Branco	Ece Suss	Friambliss	Vendemmia	Weimerund	Chardonnay	Merlot	Pinot Gris	Pinot Noir	Syrah	France	Greece	Italy	Portugal	Spain
Vintages 1954															
1958															
1962															
1966															
1970															
Countries France															
Greece															
Italy															
Portugal															
Spain															
Types Chardonnay															
Merlot															
Pinot Gris															
Pinot Noir															
Syrah															

Vintages	Wines	Types	Countries
1954			
1958			
1962			
1966			
1970			

Answers on page 370.

Stolen Street Signs

Someone's been stealing street signs in Starrington! Every week (always on a Saturday night) a new sign has gone missing. Each time it's a different type of sign (stop sign, yield sign, etc.) in a different part of town. Help the police track down the thief by matching each sign to the date it went missing and its original location at the intersection of two streets.

1. Of the speed limit sign and the one that was at Barnacle Road, one went missing on July 25th and the other was at the corner of Tarragon Lane.

2. Quinella Street doesn't intersect with Falstaff St.

3. The speed limit sign was stolen sometime after the one from Ralston Avenue.

4. The Amble Lane sign didn't go missing on August 1st.

5. The Dwight Street sign went missing one week before the one from Tarragon Lane.

6. The one-way sign was stolen 1 week before the Casper Boulevard sign, and 3 weeks before the one on Selby Street.

7. The dead end sign, the stop sign, the one from Selby Street, and the two stolen before July 14th were five different signs.

8. One of the missing signs stood at the corner of Selby Street and Barnacle Road. Selby Street doesn't have any "No Parking" signs.

9. Peabody Lane, which has no "Dead End" signs anywhere near it, intersects with either Dwight Street or Everett Avenue (but not both).

10. The stop sign went missing sometime before the sign at Peabody Lane (but not on July 18th).

	Signs						Streets						Streets					
	Dead End	No Parking	One Way	Speed Limit	Stop	Yield	Amble Ln.	Barnacle Rd.	Casper Blvd.	Dwight St.	Everett Ave.	Falstaff St.	Oracle Rd.	Peabody Ln.	Quinella St.	Ralston Ave.	Selby St.	Tarragon Ln.
Dates July 4th																		
July 11th																		
July 18th																		
July 25th																		
August 1st																		
August 8th																		
Streets Oracle Rd.																		
Peabody Ln.																		
Quinella St.																		
Ralston Ave.																		
Selby St.																		
Tarragon Ln.																		
Streets Amble Ln.																		
Barnacle Rd.																		
Casper Blvd.																		
Dwight St.																		
Everett Ave.																		
Falstaff St.																		

Dates	Signs	Streets	Streets
July 4th			
July 11th			
July 18th			
July 25th			
August 1st			
August 8th			

215

Answers on page 370.

A Case of Identity

Every word listed is contained within the group of letters. Words can be found in a straight line horizontally, vertically, or diagonally. They may be read either forward or backward.

AFFAIR DE COUER

GASSFITTERS BALL

FENCHURCH STREET

HOSMER ANGEL

JAMES WIDIBANK

LEADENHALL

MARY SUTHERLAND

SNUFF

ST. PANCRASHOTEL

ST. SAVIOURS

UNCLE NED

```
B W X Q O O V H L D Y X G D A R L
Z W A M Y H O S M E R A N G E L E
M Q S K G C F Q I C W A H U Z O T
U L B R H G S K Y P L G O D B L O
O Y L I U A W H O R P C L E V J H
Y P U A A O P K E F E L V N G A S
O Z G M H L I H N D I I N E H M A
J E S U O N T V R R P P C L P E R
N B E M G U E I A Q O S O C P S C
U B U H S T A D K S J E O N S W N
S S B Y W F T I A X T F W U N I A
Q I R W F F V E E E X S M C U D P
M A Y A T S H I W I L H D O F I T
M Q O Y W P I O E N M C E T F B S
G A S S F I T T E R S B A L L A C
F E N C H U R C H S T R E E T N Z
T S H W L V K Q H M F N Z M B K C
```

Answers on page 371.

A Case of Identity Passage 1

Each word or phrase in all capitals in the Sherlock Holmes quotation below is contained within the group of letters. Words can be found horizontally, vertically, or diagonally. They may read either forward or backward.

"My DEAR FELLOW," said Sherlock Holmes as we sat on EITHER SIDE of the FIRE in his LODGINGS at Baker Street, "life is INFINITELY STRANGER than anything which the MIND OF MAN could INVENT. We WOULD NOT DARE to CONCEIVE the things which are really mere commonplaces of EXISTENCE. If we could fly out of that window HAND IN HAND, hover over this GREAT CITY, gently REMOVE THE ROOFS, and peep in at the QUEER THINGS which are going on, the STRANGE COINCIDENCES, the plannings, the CROSS-PURPOSES, the wonderful CHAINS OF EVENTS, working through GENERATIONS, and leading to the most outré results, it would make all fiction with its CONVENTIONALITIES and foreseen CONCLUSIONS most stale and UNPROFITABLE."

```
E I N F I N I T E L Y S T R A N G E R
L X C F D Q N C U N K H Q R N X W C B
B Y R L F K U N A M F O D N I M U O M
A L O I M C M E E Z X X H D I J K N W
T V S S T N E V E F O S N I A H C V O
I E S T I G E N E R A T I O N S L E L
F R P W O U L D N O T D A R E P L N L
O I U D Q H E J F M Z H Z D Z D O T E
R F R F Y C O N C L U S I O N S D I F
P M P J T M V D O K N S N N G S G O R
N I O X I N G M M I R G V P G K I N A
U X S K C L I P D E I X E H Y S N A E
L W E W T D N A H N I D N A H U G L D
U R S T A M C T O D U V T S O O S I L
S E C N E D I C N I O C E G N A R T S
J C K D R E V I E C N O C D L R Z I X
X Q H N G S F O O R E H T E V O M E R
K Y I N I P U G R Z V Q B Y O Z C S T
U P E C N E T S I X E R I L I U S T O
```

Answers on page 371.

A Case of Identity Passage 2

Each word or phrase in all capitals in the Sherlock Holmes quotation below is contained within the group of letters. Words can be found horizontally, vertically, or diagonally. They may read either forward or backward.

INDEED, I have found that it is USUALLY in UNIMPORTANT matters that there is a FIELD for the OBSERVATION, and for the QUICK ANALYSIS of CAUSE AND EFFECT which gives the CHARM to an INVESTIGATION. The LARGER CRIMES are apt to be the SIMPLER, for the BIGGER the crime the more OBVIOUS, as a rule, is the MOTIVE. In these cases, save for one rather INTRICATE MATTER which has been REFERRED TO ME from MARSEILLES, there is nothing which PRESENTS any FEATURES of interest. It is possible, however, that I may have something better before VERY MANY MINUTES are over, for this is one of my CLIENTS, or I am much MISTAKEN."

```
G P I N T R I C A T E M A T T E R M Y
H S I S Y L A N A K C I U Q M I E O M
S E L L I E S R A M M S B K C C F T I
V X L B P M F S G Z B T X I W Y E I B
A E A I D R I O G Z W A A V G N R V P
J O R L D A E N H M J K Q T E G R E I
B N G Y V H B S V G A E T N R V E N W
N J E X M C S P E E W N S K N S D R N
O F R N R A A Y F N S C U L N E T L I
I E C G I F N G S U T T O L E M O Y Z
T A R O M O V Y I C V S I D T Q M M J
A T I F V D D A M L K D V G G Y E G Q
V U M A P X H Y P I K V B F A Y U L A
R R E Z Y W L S L E N E O N I T H Y Z
E E S W C L V K E N Q U M X C E I K V
S S V D A W Y L R T G Q T C R P L O I
B J A U Y I V T F S W B B E Y E P D N
O Y S U N I M P O R T A N T S T J Z D
R U C A U S E A N D E F F E C T A P W
```

Answers on page 371.

A Case of Identity Passage 3

Each word or phrase in all capitals in the Sherlock Holmes quotation below is contained within the group of letters. Words can be found horizontally, vertically, or diagonally. They may read either forward or backward.

Well, she had a SLATE-COLOURED, broad-brimmed STRAW HAT, with a FEATHER of a BRICKISH RED. Her JACKET was black, with BLACK BEADS sewn upon it, and a FRINGE of little black jet ORNAMENTS. Her dress was brown, rather darker than COFFEE COLOUR, with a little PURPLE PLUSH at the neck and SLEEVES. Her GLOVES were GREYISH and were WORN THROUGH at the right FOREFINGER. Her boots I didn't observe. She had small round, hanging GOLD EARRINGS, and a GENERAL AIR of being fairly WELL-TO-DO in a VULGAR, comfortable, EASY-GOING way."

```
V E K Q M H W N L H F I M S K L P
E L A Z C O F F E E C O L O U R R
G L D N Y E G P Q E B R N V E I T
N V W Q H O R E H T A E F G A E I
I E O K F R S G T G A I N L K B D
R A R Z U N C D L V N I A C E T D
F S N W K A A U A S F R A Y U A E
A Y T E F M V R G E E J O L P H R
X G H L N E G X R N B V U L V W H
V O R L M N C O E P A K E V D A S
U I O T H T F G D E E F C E A R I
V N U O F S U F Q Z D O L A L T K
B G G D E R U O L O C E T A L S C
U W H O Z M Z X H S I Y E R G B I
S H Q O Y X D H A B G L O V E S R
I O V R S G N I R R A E D L O G B
P U R P L E P L U S H U W M G Y V
```

Answers on page 371.

A Case of Identity Passage 4

Each word or phrase in all capitals in the Sherlock Holmes quotation below is contained within the group of letters. Words can be found horizontally, vertically, or diagonally. They may read either forward or backward.

PON MY WORD, Watson, you are coming along WONDERFULLY. You have really done VERY WELL indeed. IT IS TRUE that you have missed EVERYTHING of IMPORTANCE, but you have HIT UPON the METHOD, and you have a QUICK EYE for COLOUR. Never TRUST to general IMPRESSIONS, my boy, but CONCENTRATE yourself upon DETAILS.

```
E C N A T R O P M I T Y E
I T I S T R U E V V S S C
P C W A X N K O K S U N O
B O O M L B C J L H R O N
L U N K E R Q I J O T I C
Q L D M F T A W E N C S E
U R E A Y T H L Z O S S N
I V R W E W R O N P U E T
C C F D Y Y O P D U S R R
K A U I C R U R E T A P A
E F L O D X E Y D I G M T
Y C L M Q C P V T H R I E
E I Y E V E R Y T H I N G
```

Answers on page 372.

A Case of Identity Passage 5

Each word or phrase in all capitals in the Sherlock Holmes quotation below is contained within the group of letters. Words can be found horizontally, vertically, or diagonally. They may read either forward or backward.

"THE LAW cannot, as you say, TOUCH YOU," said Holmes, UNLOCKING and THROWING OPEN the door, "yet there never was a man who deserved PUNISHMENT more. If the YOUNG LADY has a BROTHER or a friend, he ought to LAY A WHIP across your SHOULDERS. By Jove!" he CONTINUED, flushing up at the sight of the BITTER SNEER upon the man's face, "it is not part of my DUTIES to my CLIENT, but here's a HUNTING CROP handy, and I think I shall just TREAT MYSELF to–" He took TWO SWIFT STEPS to the WHIP, but before he could grasp it there was a WILD CLATTER of steps upon the STAIRS, the HEAVY HALL DOOR banged, and from the window we could see Mr. James Windibank running at the TOP OF HIS SPEED down the road.

"There's a COLD-BLOODED SCOUNDREL!" said Holmes, laughing, as he threw himself down into his chair once more. "That fellow will rise from CRIME TO CRIME until he does something very bad, and ends on a GALLOWS. The case has, in SOME RESPECTS, been not entirely DEVOID OF INTEREST."

```
V C O L D B L O O D E D S C O U N D R E L
D M D N S P E T S T F I W S O W T T B B X
S U D F L L C G Y E M I R C O T E M I R C
I I T Q G W Q D N R R I E A H B B E Q O T
U L Q I B Z I V R I A S H O U L D E R S N
O W H J E L L M K T K F K L E M E E E D E
X C O E Z S O H S G S C L P U R G K E E I
N H S W O L L A G C R H O O G R M V T B L
H E U T L A Y A W H I P T L D K O D T I C
E U P O R C G N I T N U H Q N I E S R T Y
A D D O Y X C U R B W T X U D U T E E T X
V D P N G H D E U N I T N O C C L Y A E B
Y D U Q L N C V C F J I F J E O D M T R H
H T N D D C I U V E Q I N P W A I L M S C
A H I X B G Z W O F N M S Q L Z V W Y N X
L E S B D M B R O T H E R G J B H W S E G
L L H Z E H F W E R R U N R Z I J P E E V
D A M L K P O R A E H U F X P O A G L R Q
O W E H U I E Q M R O T L A Y X T J F H M
O Z N F T S H O N Y W I L D C L A T T E R
R S T N T H S T O P O F H I S S P E E D U
```

Answers on page 372.

The Master Forger

The art world is agog! Six recently-sold paintings, each supposed to be by the hand of a different world-famous artist, have now been conclusively shown to be forgeries. Authorities believe the same "master forger" is behind all of this but they're still not sure who he or she actually is. Using only the clues available below, match each forged painting to the artist it was claimed to have been painted by, the country it was sold in, and the price it fetched at auction.

1. The Hal Garrison piece sold for four times as much money as "Cold Hills."

2. "Forever Blue" sold for twice as much as the painting sold in Portugal.

3. Of the piece that sold for $8,000,000 and the Inga Howell painting, one was "Cold Hills" and the other was sold in France.

4. The Inga Howell forgery wasn't sold in Spain.

5. "Baby Jane" (which wasn't passed off as a Margot Lane painting) fetched less money at auction than the piece that was sold in Portugal.

6. Of the painting sold in Germany and "Eighteen," one sold for 32 million dollars and the other was alleged to have been an early work by Greta Frank.

7. The Lyle Kramer painting fetched more money at auction than "Forever Blue," which was said to have been a Hal Garrison piece.

8. "Day of Night," the piece that sold for $2,000,000, and the painting that was sold in Norway were three different forgeries.

9. "Awestruck" didn't sell for either $2 million or $4 million.

10. The Freda Estes painting sold for $16,000,000, but not in Norway.

	Paintings						Countries						Artists					
	Awestruck	Baby Jane	Cold Hills	Day of Night	Eighteen	Forever Blue	Canada	France	Germany	Norway	Portugal	Spain	Freda Estes	Greta Frank	Hal Garrison	Inga Howell	Lyle Kramer	Margot Lane
Prices																		
$1,000,000																		
$2,000,000																		
$4,000,000																		
$8,000,000																		
$16,000,000																		
$32,000,000																		
Artists																		
Freda Estes																		
Greta Frank																		
Hal Garrison																		
Inga Howell																		
Lyle Kramer																		
Margot Lane																		
Countries																		
Canada																		
France																		
Germany																		
Norway																		
Portugal																		
Spain																		

Prices	Paintings	Countries	Artists
$1,000,000			
$2,000,000			
$4,000,000			
$8,000,000			
$16,000,000			
$32,000,000			

Answers on page 372.

Witness Statements

There was a break-in at Sal's jewelry store last night! Police have interviewed five people who claimed to have witnessed the theft, but their stories vary quite a bit. Help the police sort out their statements by matching each witness report to the correct height and weight of the person they saw, and the type of car in which they made their getaway.

1. Of the person Gerald saw and the 190-pound suspect, one was 5'2" and the other drove a Nissan.

2. The man Russell saw was 3 inches shorter than whoever was driving the Toyota, and 6 inches shorter than the 135-pound suspect.

3. Yolanda's suspect was either 5'2" or 5'8" tall.

4. The 190-pound suspect was nine inches shorter than whoever was driving the Mazda.

5. The man driving the Honda appeared to be 5'8" tall.

6. Angela's suspect wasn't 5'5" tall or 160 pounds.

7. The 145-pound suspect wasn't 5'11", and didn't drive the Nissan.

		Witnesses					Weights					Cars				
		Angela S.	Gerald F.	Russell T.	Sarah M.	Yolanda V.	135 lbs	145 lbs	160 lbs	190 lbs	225 lbs	Chevrolet	Honda	Mazda	Nissan	Toyota
Heights	5' 2"															
	5' 5"															
	5' 8"															
	5' 11"															
	6' 2"															
Cars	Chevrolet															
	Honda															
	Mazda															
	Nissan															
	Toyota															
Weights	135 lbs															
	145 lbs															
	160 lbs															
	190 lbs															
	225 lbs															

Heights	Witnesses	Weights	Cars
5' 2"			
5' 5"			
5' 8"			
5' 11"			
6' 2"			

Answers on page 372.

The Adventure of the Copper Beeches Letter Pt. 1

Each word or phrase in all capitals in the Sherlock Holmes quotation below is contained within the group of letters. Words can be found horizontally, vertically, or diagonally. They may read either forward or backward.

Dear Miss Hunter:—Miss Stoper has very KINDLY given me your ADDRESS, and I write from here to ask you whether you have RECONSIDERED your DECISION. My wife is very ANXIOUS that you should come, for she has been much ATTRACTED by my DESCRIPTION of you. We are WILLING to give £30 a quarter, or £120 a year, so as to RECOMPENSE you for any little INCONVENIENCE which our fads may cause you. They are not very EXACTING, after all. My wife is fond of a PARTICULAR shade of ELECTRIC BLUE and would like you to wear such a dress INDOORS in the MORNING. You need not, however, go to the expense of PURCHASING one, as we have one BELONGING to my dear daughter ALICE (now in PHILADELPHIA), which would, I should think, fit you very well.

```
E L E C T R I C B L U E P R D
J G N I S A H C R U P A B A E
E N A T T R A C T E D N G L S
W I U S D K T C N B S X I U C
D G G N I T C A X E C I U C R
G N I L L I W D I K Y O Y I I
L O E B Q E E K N G C U L T P
N L N H W C L C D H A S D R T
W E J C I E H H O V Z L N A I
N B E S N E P M O C E R I P O
G N I N R O M U R N D C K C N
X O P H N E C S S E R D D A E
N M I N C O N V E N I E N C E
R E C O N S I D E R E D W Q H
P H I L A D E L P H I A Z D Y
```

Answers on page 372.

The Adventure of the Copper Beeches Letter Pt. 2

Each word or phrase in all capitals in the Sherlock Holmes quotation below is contained within the group of letters. Words can be found horizontally, vertically, or diagonally. They may read either forward or backward.

Then, as to SITTING here or there, or AMUSING YOURSELF in any MANNER indicated, that need cause you no INCONVENIENCE. As regards your HAIR, it is no doubt a PITY, especially as I could not help REMARKING its BEAUTY during our SHORT INTERVIEW, but I am AFRAID that I must REMAIN FIRM upon this point, and I only hope that the INCREASED SALARY may RECOMPENSE you for the LOSS. Your DUTIES, as far as the child is CONCERNED, are VERY LIGHT. Now do try to come, and I shall meet you with the DOG-CART at WINCHESTER. Let me know your train. Yours FAITHFULLY, JEPHRO RUCASTLE.

```
H X M Y X Y P E S O L X V E E H Z
A J R J W L A M M I Y L V C G A S
I K I J E L S Y Z T T N N N N S
R E F J I U W T V U R T I E O L O
E S N B V F K U X V C K I I G D L
T N I E R H M A B X R F Q N D D X
S E A W E T F E A A I S D E G S G
E P M Y T I P B M D M S N V A Z U
H M E Y N A V E N J N R O N F V V
C O R U I F R C M S E B J O R E R
N C R W T M E W A C D O G C A R T
I E W T R T Z J N B X H L N I Y S
W R X X O K H O N Z N O E I D L E
J R A H H E C B E A L X I C T I I
R E L T S A C U R O R H P E J G T
I N C R E A S E D S A L A R Y H U
A M U S I N G Y O U R S E L F T D
```

Answers on page 372.

Adventure of the Copper Beeches Passage 1

Each word or phrase in all capitals in the Sherlock Holmes quotation below is contained within the group of letters. Words can be found horizontally, vertically, or diagonally. They may read either forward or backward.

"DO YOU KNOW, Watson," said he, "that it is one of the CURSES of a MIND with a turn like mine that I must look at EVERYTHING with REFERENCE to my own SPECIAL SUBJECT. You look at these SCATTERED HOUSES, and you are IMPRESSED by their BEAUTY. I look at them, and the only thought which comes to me is a FEELING of their ISOLATION and of the IMPUNITY with which crime may be COMMITTED there."

"GOOD HEAVENS!" I cried. "Who would ASSOCIATE crime with these dear old HOMESTEADS?"

"They always fill me with a CERTAIN HORROR. It is my belief, Watson, FOUNDED upon my EXPERIENCE, that the LOWEST AND VILEST alleys in London do not present a more dreadful RECORD OF SIN than does the SMILING and beautiful COUNTRYSIDE."

"You HORRIFY me!"

```
O Y G T C E J B U S L A I C E P S G S
L M N X S C A T T E R E D H O U S E S
Z R I G H E Q E D S Y T B S D Q E S B
B S H P P X Y G J R F E V F E Z U N X
H I T F N P O N K U G N I L I M S E D
W R Y Z R E C I P C H R M T Z E I V F
N J R Z W R O L K G W I P D C S A A A
D E E N O I M E G F S M R N L Y B E C
N T V P N E M E E O W E E M M V C H O
I A E S K N I F L B X R S D T E Q D U
S I N I U C T A O U E W S V R Y N O N
F C L M O E T B B F J B E X T I Q O T
O O Q P Y I E Q E J X B D U M M B G R
D S U U O H D R W W Z A A P J N A F Y
R S Z N D S D A E T S E M O H C U Q S
O A I I D Q R D N S B H O R R I F Y I
C B C T C E R T A I N H O R R O R N D
E P L Y G T D G K W Z M T Q X P P O E
R L O W E S T A N D V I L E S T L Y T
```

Answers on page 373.

Describing Sherlock Holmes

Cryptograms are messages in substitution code. Break the code to read the message. For example, THE SMART CAT might become FVO QWGDF JGF if **F** is substituted for **T**, **V** for **H**, **O** for **E**, and so on. Bonus: Who is the speaker of this quote? Which story is the source of the quote?

"JM JK ACM RZKW MC RUEIRKK MLR JARUEIRK-KJXDR," LR ZAKSRIRT SJML Z DZONL. "LCDBRK JK Z DJMMDR MCC KVJRAMJPJV PCI BW MZK-MRK–JM ZEEICZVLRK MC VCDT-XDCCTRTARKK. J VCODT JBZNJAR LJK NJQJAR Z PIJRAT Z DJM-MDR EJAVL CP MLR DZMRKM QRNRMZXDR ZDFZDCJT, ACM COM CP BZDRQCDRAVR, WCO OATRIKMZAT, XOM KJBEDW COM CP Z KEJIJM CP JAGOJIW JA CITRI MC LZQR ZA ZVVOIZMR JTRZ CP MLR RPPRVMK. MC TC LJB HOKMJVR, J MLJAF MLZM LR SCODT MZFR JM LJBKRDP SJML MLR KZBR IRZTJARKK. LR ZEERZIK MC LZQR Z EZKKJCA PCI TRPJAJMR ZAT RUZVM FACSDRTNR."

What Changed? (Part I)

The consulting detective was at a house party. What did she see in the kitchen? Examine the objects, then turn the page.

What Changed? (Part II)

Someone was found unconscious at the house party! They said they'd spotted an intruder and then everything went dark. The consulting detective immediately spotted that one object changed position, and that object was found to be the hastily cleaned weapon. From memory, can you work out what changed position?

What Went Missing? (Part I)

The consulting detective met with a nature photographer and writer who had received strange threatening messages. Examine the objects on the writer's desk, then turn the page.

What Went Missing? (Part II)

The next day, the writer was hit over the head and rushed to the hospital. The consulting detective went to the scene and immediately spotted that something had been stolen. From memory, can you work out what went missing?

Words of a Genius

Cryptograms are messages in substitution code. Break the code to read the message. For example, THE SMART CAT might become FVO QWGDF JGF if **F** is substituted for **T, V** for **H, O** for **E,** and so on. Bonus: Who is the speaker of the quote? Which story is the source of the quote?

"ZPO YO YL D JPWLOYGF GM HWOOYFH SWODY-

AL. HYRW EW VGPK SWODYAL, DFS MKGE DF

DKEBCDYK Y TYAA KWOPKF VGP DF WUB-

WAAWFO WUIWKO GIYFYGF. ZPO OG KPF

CWKW DFS KPF OCWKW, OG BKGLL-JPWLOYGF

KDYATDV HPDKSL, DFS AYW GF EV MDBW TYOC

D AWFL OG EV WVW–YO YL FGO EV EWOYWK.

FG, VGP DKW OCW GFW EDF TCG BDF BAWDK

OCW EDOOWK PI. YM VGP CDRW D MDFBV

OG LWW VGPK FDEW YF OCW FWUO CGFGPKL

AYLO–"

Answers on page 373.

Bank Robberies

Bledsoe County has been beset by a gang of bank robbers! Five different banks, each in a different town, have been robbed by the same gang in just the past 10 days. The total amount stolen from each bank was never the same, and the gang never robbed more than one bank on any given day. Using only the clues below, help track down the gang by matching each bank to the town it is in, and determine the date each was robbed as well as how much was stolen.

1. The most expensive robbery happened 2 days after Bell Largo was hit.

2. The gang got away with $4,800 2 days before they robbed another bank of $2,500.

3. Of Apex Bank and Wellspring, one was robbed on June 11th and the other lost $4,800.

4. The bank in Grumley was either Wellspring or the one robbed on June 9th.

5. Bell Largo was robbed 2 days before the bank in Cold Spring.

6. The $1,000 robbery took place 2 days before Moneycorp was hit, but not in Yountville.

7. The gang robbed a bank (which wasn't Apex) in Tahoe on June 7th.

8. Cold Spring's bank was robbed on June 11th.

	Banks					Towns					Amounts				
	Apex	Bell Largo	First Trust	Moneycorp	Wellspring	Cold Spring	Grumley	Longwood	Tahoe	Yountville	$1,000	$1,600	$2,500	$4,800	$10,200
Dates June 3															
June 5															
June 7															
June 9															
June 11															
Amounts $1,000															
$1,600															
$2,500															
$4,800															
$10,200															
Towns Cold Spring															
Grumley															
Longwood															
Tahoe															
Yountville															

Dates	Banks	Towns	Amounts
June 3			
June 5			
June 7			
June 9			
June 11			

245

Answers on page 373.

The Adventure of the Greek Interpreter

Each word or phrase in all capitals in the Sherlock Holmes quotation below is contained within the group of letters. Words can be found horizontally, vertically, or diagonally. They may read either forward or backward.

"What is to me a means of LIVELIHOOD is to him the merest HOBBY of a DILETTANTE. He has an EXTRAORDINARY faculty for figures, and AUDITS the books in some of the GOVERNMENT departments. MYCROFT lodges in Pall Mall, and he walks round the corner into WHITEHALL every morning and back every evening. From year's end to year's end he takes no other exercise, and is seen nowhere else, except only in the DIOGENES CLUB, which is just opposite his rooms."

"I cannot recall the name."

"Very likely not. There are many men in London, you know, who, some from SHYNESS, some from MISANTHROPY, have no wish for the COMPANY of their fellows. Yet they are not AVERSE to comfortable chairs and the latest PERIODICALS. It is for the convenience of these that the Diogenes Club was started, and it now contains the most UNSOCIABLE and UNCLUBABLE men in town. No MEMBER is permitted to take the least notice of any other one. Save in the STRANGER'S

ROOM, no talking is, under any circumstances, allowed, and three OFFENCES, if brought to the notice of the committee, render the talker liable to EXPULSION. My brother was one of the FOUNDERS, and I have myself found it a very SOOTHING atmosphere."

```
D Y W C U X H F S I T F O R C Y M
I R G G R Z O R L Y E Y M T M G Y
O A L V Y U B G A P A B E N O N N
G N I U N O S V C O A B T E O I A
E I V D L P E A I R U O N M R H P
N D E L F R C W D H D H A N S T M
E R L N S Z N H O T I V T R R O O
S O I E I E E I I N T Y T E E O C
C A H Z P L F T R A S L E V G S K
L R O Y G B F E E S W H L O N D O
U T O W I A O H P I H T I G A H H
B X D I U B J A R M J Y D S R Y D
R E P J N U X L I W I O N E T B U
W A F K A L A L A K A U B E S B L
E L B A I C O S N U Y M L B S I U
K V C I E N F W V F E R Y I V S S
N O I S L U P X E M X Z D L N C K
```

Answers on page 374.

The Adventure of the Norwood Builder

Each word or phrase in all capitals in the Sherlock Holmes quotation below is contained within the group of letters. Words can be found horizontally, vertically, or diagonally. They may read either forward or backward.

"From the point of view of the criminal EXPERT," said Mr. Sherlock Holmes, "London has become a singularly UNINTERESTING city since the death of the late LAMENTED Professor Moriarty."

"I can hardly think that you would find many DECENT citizens to agree with you," I answered.

"Well, well, I must not be SELFISH," said he, with a smile, as he pushed back his chair from the breakfast-table. "The COMMUNITY is certainly the gainer, and no one the loser, save the poor out-of-work SPECIALIST, whose OCCUPATION has gone. With that man in the field, one's morning paper presented INFINITE possibilities. Often it was only the smallest trace, Watson, the faintest indication, and yet it was enough to tell me that the great MALIGNANT brain was there, as the gentlest TREMORS of the edges of the web remind one of the foul spider which lurks in the centre. PETTY thefts, WANTON assaults, purposeless outrage—to the man who held the CLUE all could be worked

into one connected whole. To the SCIENTIFIC student of the higher criminal world, no capital in Europe offered the ADVANTAGES which LONDON then possessed. But now——" He shrugged his shoulders in humorous DEPRECATION of the state of things which he had himself done so much to produce.

```
N  T  T  R  E  M  O  R  S  N  F  Y  G  V  Y
O  S  H  E  U  Y  V  Y  O  Z  X  V  H  M  T
I  I  M  S  L  L  E  D  P  E  T  T  Y  U  I
T  L  U  C  C  N  F  V  Z  Q  X  L  N  N
A  A  S  I  G  O  H  S  I  F  L  E  S  I  U
C  I  M  E  L  I  H  A  D  N  X  B  V  N  M
E  C  A  N  G  T  B  N  B  A  F  K  A  T  M
R  E  L  T  I  A  F  O  G  K  C  J  I  E  O
P  P  I  I  N  P  T  T  N  E  C  E  D  R  C
E  S  G  F  F  U  A  N  R  Y  X  G  W  E  U
D  C  N  I  I  C  K  A  A  R  C  D  L  S  Q
I  W  A  C  N  C  C  W  S  V  O  Y  Z  T  C
H  W  N  M  I  O  Q  O  K  V  D  H  K  I  D
M  L  T  I  T  D  E  T  N  E  M  A  L  N  R
K  Y  Z  J  E  P  J  T  R  E  P  X  E  G  T
```

Answers on page 374.

The Reigate Puzzle

Each word or phrase in all capitals in the Sherlock Holmes quotation below is contained within the group of letters. Words can be found horizontally, vertically, or diagonally. They may read either forward or backward.

On referring to my notes I see that it was upon the 14th of April that I received a TELEGRAM from Lyons which informed me that Holmes was LYING ILL in the Hotel Dulong. Within twenty-four hours I was in his SICK-ROOM, and was relieved to find that there was nothing formidable in his SYMPTOMS. Even his iron CONSTITUTION, however, had broken down under the STRAIN of an investigation which had extended over two months, during which period he had never worked less than fifteen hours a day, and had more than once, as he assured me, kept to his TASK for five days at a stretch. Even the TRIUMPHANT issue of his labors could not save him from REACTION after so terrible an EXERTION, and at a time when Europe was ringing with his name and when his room was literally ankle-deep with CONGRATULATORY telegrams I found him a prey to the blackest DEPRESSION. Even the knowledge that he had succeeded where the police of three countries had failed, and that he had OUTMANOEUVRED at every point the most accomplished SWINDLER in Europe, was insufficient to ROUSE him from his nervous PROSTRATION.

```
N W E D N Y X T E T K A A I Q C W O R
O V K E O N F G V Y Y F O T E K Q L R
I Q D R I R C D I Y K I N S Q E G S W
T E Q V S L C V Q Z Q A W O H T E Y L
U C X U S Z L K Q H H I D S C G D M Y
T V R E E Y P B O P N N E Q Y O X P I
I Z M O R B A H M D V O V R P W F T N
T Q P N P T R U L D S I O N E S L O G
S J L A E T I E U L D T Z T I M B M I
N G A M D R R O M W A A X L B A L S L
O I B T T E X K N L Z R E A N R R H L
C O Z U R K Q T U S H T F M V G S T Q
R I W O Z E I T Y W E S Q H B E I N S
K A U F T O A F G K M O V E W L C D I
S S D J W R I C Z D Y R H P U E K M H
E Y P F G K F W T D R P W K G T R L Z
O G G N G S M B F I D F T A S K O X N
J L O K I S V U S T O V V W E W O S Q
G C S C J K J E E E K N D S M N M X C
```

Answers on page 374.

Fingerprint Match

There are 8 sets of fingerprints. Find each match.

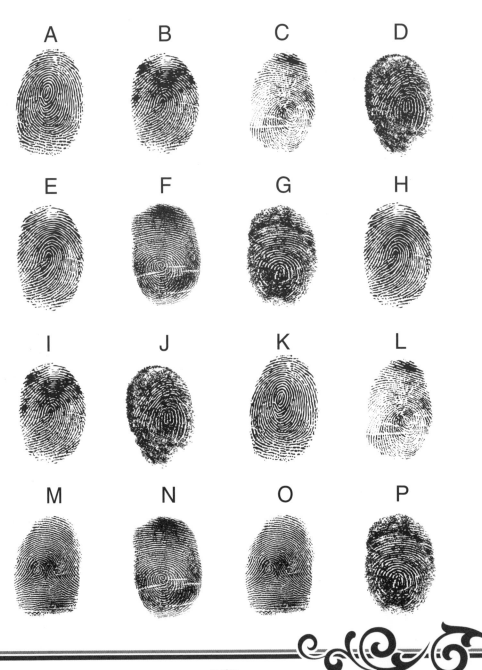

What Went Missing? (Part I)

The consulting detective met his client on Thursday about a set of thefts. The detective toured the house, including the kitchen. Examine the room, then turn the page.

Overnight, more things were stolen. The consulting detective returned to the house and figured out immediately what had gone missing. From memory, can you work out what went missing?

What Do You See? (Part I)

Study this picture of the crime scene for 1 minute, then turn the page.

What Do You See? (Part II)

(Do not read this until you have read the previous page!) Which image exactly matches the crime scene?

1

2

3

4

Answers on page 374.

What Went Missing? (Part I)

The consulting detective visited the dressing room of the actress who had received threats. Examine the objects, then turn the page.

What Went Missing? (Part II)

Overnight, the actress got sick from poison and was rushed to the hospital! The consulting detective noted something missing from her dressing room and suspected it contained the poison. From memory, can you work out what went missing?

What Went Missing? (Part I)

The consulting detective visited a client's rooms one day. What did he see? Examine the objects, then turn the page.

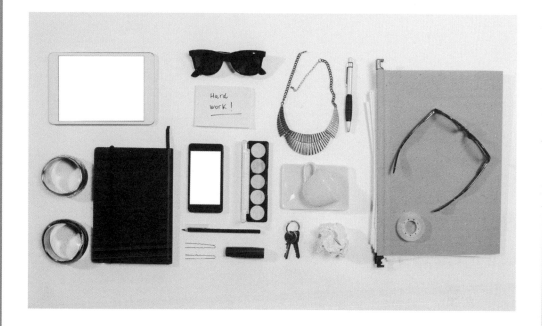

What Went Missing? (Part II)

The next day, the client went missing. Called in to help, the consulting detective saw that something else went missing as well. From memory, can you work out what went missing?

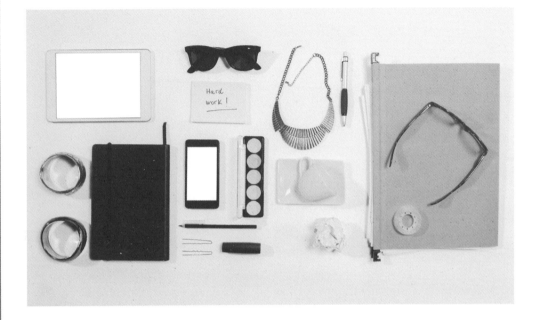

Fingerprint Match

There are 4 sets of fingerprints. Find each match.

A

B

C

D

E

F

G

H

Answers on page 375.

The Bascombe Valley Mystery

Every word listed is contained within the group of letters. Words can be found in a straight line horizontally, vertically, or diagonally. They may be read either forward or backward.

ALICE

AUSTRALIA

BALLARAT

BOSCOMBE VALLEY

CHARLES MCCARTHY

COOEE

HATHERLY FARM

HEREFORDSHIRE

JAMES

JOHN TURNER

LESTRADE

MURDER

POOL

```
E  B  O  S  C  O  M  B  E  V  A  L  L  E  Y
R  V  P  N  Y  Y  L  K  O  B  D  J  P  S  H
I  W  B  C  J  F  Y  V  G  A  L  I  C  E  T
H  R  E  N  R  U  T  N  H  O  J  T  M  Y  R
S  Z  M  A  X  W  V  F  S  M  M  A  R  K  A
D  P  A  S  U  R  W  W  K  U  Y  R  A  V  C
R  V  L  Z  H  S  E  P  O  X  H  A  F  C  C
O  J  E  E  L  W  T  D  Q  Q  Y  L  Y  C  M
F  C  E  P  S  W  U  R  R  Z  Q  L  L  C  S
E  N  E  U  T  T  X  U  A  U  P  A  R  Q  E
R  B  N  P  E  S  R  I  T  L  M  B  E  C  L
E  Q  N  P  E  P  M  A  P  T  I  A  H  O  R
H  S  O  M  O  E  L  N  D  Q  J  A  T  O  A
S  O  A  F  H  G  J  T  G  E  B  B  A  E  H
L  J  O  N  P  F  U  U  X  V  Y  W  H  E  C
```

Answers on page 375.

The Bascombe Valley Mystery Passage 1

Each word or phrase in all capitals in the Sherlock Holmes quotation below is contained within the group of letters. Words can be found horizontally, vertically, or diagonally. They may read either forward or backward.

The LARGEST landed PROPRIETOR in that part is a Mr. JOHN TURNER, who made his MONEY in Australia and returned SOME YEARS AGO to the OLD COUNTRY. One of the farms which he held, that of HATHERLEY, was let to Mr. Charles McCarthy, who was also an ex-Australian. The men had known each other in the COLONIES, so that it was not UNNATURAL that when they came to SETTLE DOWN they should do so as near each other as POSSIBLE. Turner was apparently the RICHER MAN, so McCarthy became his tenant but still REMAINED, it seems, upon terms of PERFECT EQUALITY, as they were FREQUENTLY together.

```
N  L  F  L  U  L  Y  G  O  Q  G  I  N  R  D  Z  N
W  Z  D  B  C  O  L  D  C  O  U  N  T  R  Y  L  D
P  S  I  N  N  U  Y  L  T  N  E  U  Q  E  R  F  Y
O  U  E  Y  Y  W  H  T  C  D  L  L  R  X  S  E  D
S  K  V  O  V  C  O  Y  U  Z  H  E  R  E  L  L  O
S  Z  M  Y  M  L  T  D  R  H  M  L  I  R  R  T  Q
I  G  W  G  Q  G  A  F  E  A  W  N  E  A  I  J  O
B  B  T  L  T  U  F  Z  I  L  O  H  B  J  C  V  Z
L  A  R  U  T  A  N  N  U  L  T  H  G  G  H  K  K
E  K  R  J  M  Y  E  N  O  A  P  T  M  B  E  A  Y
I  O  C  S  O  D  Q  C  H  Y  C  R  E  L  R  W  C
I  R  R  E  N  R  U  T  N  H  O  J  A  S  M  S  O
Z  R  O  T  E  I  R  P  O  R  P  R  K  O  A  A  N
Y  N  R  W  Y  P  F  G  N  L  G  R  S  E  N  L  D
G  C  P  E  R  F  E  C  T  E  Q  U  A  L  I  T  Y
X  G  A  C  X  O  G  A  S  R  A  E  Y  E  M  O  S
A  O  O  U  W  E  I  T  W  J  H  G  Z  K  S  J  L
```

Answers on page 375.

The Bascombe Valley Mystery Passage 2

Each word or phrase in all capitals in the Sherlock Holmes quotation below is contained within the group of letters. Words can be found horizontally, vertically, or diagonally. They may read either forward or backward.

"In view of YOUR HEALTH, nothing. You are yourself AWARE that you will soon have to ANSWER for your DEED at a HIGHER COURT than the ASSIZES. I will keep your CONFESSION, and if McCarthy is condemned I shall be FORCED to use it. If not, it shall never be seen by MORTAL EYE; and your SECRET, whether you be ALIVE OR DEAD, shall be SAFE WITH US."

```
H I G H E R C O U R T D T
S S A F E W I T H U S C N
E J S O M U E D Z H F O F
Z B F R B A E T T C I K E
I B W C D K Z L S S L V Y
S E O E C S A M S M Q I E
S J A D O E E E C L G H L
A V S N H H F C L U D A A
L X G R S N V P R E W W T
V F U A O W K I E E Y A R
H O T C M L E D Y F T R O
Y P C R B M R R L X B E M
A L I V E O R D E A D L P
```

Answers on page 375.

The Bascombe Valley
Mystery Passage 3

Each word or phrase in all capitals in the Sherlock Holmes quotation below is contained within the group of letters. Words can be found horizontally, vertically, or diagonally. They may read either forward or backward.

It was with his BARMAID WIFE that he had spent the LAST THREE

DAYS in BRISTOL, and his FATHER did not know where he was.

MARK THAT POINT. It is of IMPORTANCE. Good has come out of

EVIL, however, for the barmaid, finding from the PAPERS that he is in

SERIOUS TROUBLE and likely to be HANGED, has thrown him over

UTTERLY and has written to him to say that she has a HUSBAND

already in the BERMUDA DOCKYARD, so that there is really no tie

BETWEEN them. I think that that BIT OF NEWS has CONSOLED

young MCCARTHY for all that he has SUFFERED."

```
H R P A H P C L S U I X Y D J M N
A D E L O S N O C E C I N L S J F
N D E H I T K Z V U F R H B Y C I
G V S R Q E F I W D I A M R A B B
E L L Q E X L F L Y U Y T E D C E
D B I T O F N E W S O L K H E A T
M H I E O T F U T C X R B P E I W
C S E M G K R U U E S E K R R R E
C A P A P E R S S U Y T Q G H C E
A V H F O O M B R I S T O L T G N
R U I T R O R N I K C U R T T Q B
T E L B U O R T S U O I R E S L I
H D N A B S U H A O G L J Y A O L
Y P J U L I I G Y N W Z J D L V Y
U B E R M U D A D O C K Y A R D T
E X R W X C P O J C B E Q T E E S
Y K N U T N I O P T A H T K R A M
```

Answers on page 376.

The Con Artist

The F.B.I. has been on the hunt for a con artist accused of swindling thousands of dollars from his victims. His real name is Barney Green, but he routinely jumps from place to place using a new assumed name whenever he moves to a new location. Barney always creates a new fake "career" for each of his identities, and he never kept the same identity for more than a month. Help the F.B.I. track Mr. Green's latest movements by matching each name he used to its correct location and month, and determine the "career" he invented for each fake identity.

1. Of the "Fred Flores" identity and whichever name Barney used in Trippany, one was supposedly a doctor and the other was used in July.

2. Mr. Green didn't pass himself off as a lawyer while he was using the name "Pat Perry."

3. Barney pretended to be an accountant one month and a bank manager during another. One of those two identities was "Abe Avery". The other was the one he used in June.

4. He pretended to be "Sean Starr" sometime after he passed himself off as an accountant.

5. The F.B.I. know two of Barney's fake names were "Abe Avery" and "Matt Mintz," and that of those two, he used one in the city of Valero and he used the other in May.

6. Barney was in the town of Hoople either in August or in whichever month he pretended to be a dentist (but not both).

7. Mr. Green claimed to be a reporter one month before he was in Beaverton. Sometime after he left Beaverton he used the name "Pat Perry".

8. We know for a fact that Barney was pretending to be a doctor during his time in Opalville, and that he was in Nanaimo in May.

9. He never used the name "Lou Lemon" during his time in Beaverton, and he didn't pass himself off as an accountant in April.

	Names						Towns						Careers					
	Abe Avery	Fred Flores	Lou Lemon	Matt Mintz	Pat Perry	Sean Starr	Beaverton	Hoople	Nanaimo	Opalville	Trippany	Valero	Accountant	Bank mgr.	Dentist	Doctor	Lawyer	Reporter
Months March																		
April																		
May																		
June																		
July																		
August																		
Careers Accountant																		
Bank mgr.																		
Dentist																		
Doctor																		
Lawyer																		
Reporter																		
Towns Beaverton																		
Hoople																		
Nanaimo																		
Opalville																		
Trippany																		
Valero																		

Months	Names	Towns	Careers
March			
April			
May			
June			
July			
August			

Answers on page 376.

The Adventure of the Speckled Band

Every word listed is contained within the group of letters. Words can be found in a straight line horizontally, vertically, or diagonally. They may be read either forward or backward.

ARMITAGE	SPECKLED BAND
BABOON	STEPFATHER
CALCUTTA	STOKE MORAN
CHEETAH	SURREY
FARINTOSH	SWAMP ADDER
HELEN STONER	TWINS
HONORIA	VENTILATOR
GRIMESBY ROYLOTT	WESTPHAIL
SNAKE	

```
G  R  I  M  E  S  B  Y  R  O  Y  L  O  T  T
R  S  T  O  K  E  M  O  R  A  N  D  B  S  V
R  O  H  E  L  E  N  S  T  O  N  E  R  P  R
G  B  T  F  A  R  I  N  T  O  S  H  E  E  E
K  F  A  A  O  K  U  K  J  B  M  A  H  C  D
N  Q  A  B  L  U  K  S  P  Q  I  T  F  K  D
G  L  T  G  O  I  C  Q  L  R  A  E  N  L  A
A  I  T  I  X  O  T  H  O  F  I  F  L  E  P
R  A  U  X  H  I  N  N  P  J  W  G  S  D  M
M  H  C  Y  Y  A  O  E  E  D  I  N  Q  B  A
I  P  L  Y  E  H  T  T  G  V  A  C  H  A  W
T  T  A  U  R  S  M  E  A  K  T  W  I  N  S
A  S  C  Z  R  K  M  R  E  X  W  A  T  D  L
G  E  T  G  U  A  G  K  A  H  Z  W  Y  F  N
E  W  B  E  S  N  B  K  E  F  C  T  F  H  V
```

Answers on page 376.

The Adventure of
the Speckled Band Story Pt. 1

Each word or phrase in all capitals in the Sherlock Holmes quotation below is contained within the group of letters. Words can be found horizontally, vertically, or diagonally. They may read either forward or backward.

"The family was at one time AMONG THE RICHEST in England, and the ESTATES extended over the BORDERS into BERKSHIRE in the north, and HAMPSHIRE in the west. In the LAST CENTURY, however, four SUCCESSIVE HEIRS were of a DISSOLUTE and WASTEFUL DISPOSITION, and the FAMILY RUIN was eventually COMPLETED by a GAMBLER in the days of the REGENCY. Nothing was left save a FEW ACRES of ground, and the TWO-HUNDRED-YEAR-OLD house, which is itself CRUSHED under a HEAVY MORTGAGE."

```
A M O N G T H E R I C H E S T M I H E
W A S T E F U L D I S P O S I T I O N
Y W V B B F U C H Q A U R K C N B Z R
C O Q T S M E T L K O G E E N M P T D
N J Z H E J M W E V J N J Z L O C L U
E D H I R D P R A W U E B B T B O H Q
G K E E I P I M X C M O E R Y H M C G
E N A T H H K S F D R E R V R D P A A
R C V L S S Y B S D C E Q S U E L W G
N B Y P K Z L B E O A Y S A T H E H I
P U M M R P M R M B L U W G N S T K W
W A O A E H S L T E H U U Z E U E C G
H Q R C B Z O O Q Z Y W T G C R D S T
Q E T B R N J V G W K F D E T C E U E
X T G J L O L D S H Z Q D D S T B X E
P E A N I U R Y L I M A F V A P F B U
Y Y G F B N P P T I Q Q K T L E C I I
D Q E S R I E H E V I S S E C C U S A
T W O H U N D R E D Y E A R O L D T P
```

Answers on page 376.

The Adventure of the Speckled Band Story Pt. 2

Each word or phrase in all capitals in the Sherlock Holmes quotation below is contained within the group of letters. Words can be found horizontally, vertically, or diagonally. They may read either forward or backward.

"The LAST SQUIRE dragged out his EXISTENCE there, living the HORRIBLE LIFE of an ARISTOCRATIC pauper; but his only son, my STEPFATHER, seeing that he must ADAPT himself to the new conditions, OBTAINED an advance from a RELATIVE, which ENABLED him to take a MEDICAL DEGREE and went out to CALCUTTA, where, by his PROFESSIONAL skill and his FORCE OF CHARACTER, he established a LARGE PRACTICE. In a FIT OF ANGER, however, caused by some ROBBERIES which had been PERPETRATED in the house, he beat his native BUTLER to death and narrowly escaped a CAPITAL SENTENCE. As it was, he suffered a long term of IMPRISONMENT and afterwards RETURNED to England a MOROSE and DISAPPOINTED man."

```
X W V J C A P I T A L S E N T E N C E
V O T P A D A I I G T P O E A L M M Y
J S M E E V D E N R U T E R B N O E D
H Q V V X V D U B H U X U E U E R D E
L G O I Y M U E O E M R C C T N O I T
L A S T S Q U I R E Q I B Y L K S C A
H G L A S T E P F A T H E R E A E A R
R C M L R G X I X C B C T P R C C L T
E O M E L R G P A K F W X M Q U Y D E
N S B R I M P R I S O N M E N T F E P
A M E B N O P E E D N Z M X D D I G R
B E Y B E E F I T O F A N G E R U R E
L P Z R G R F O E X I S T E N C E E P
E I D R K J I H A T Q M V Z I W L E S
D R A F O R C E O F C H A R A C T E R
Y L K C W A R I S T O C R A T I C N H
D I S A P P O I N T E D O N B R L U L
H O R R I B L E L I F E V C O L M W D
P R O F E S S I O N A L H W C W O Q R
```

Answers on page 376.

The Adventure of the Speckled Band Story Pt. 3

Each word or phrase in all capitals in the Sherlock Holmes quotation below is contained within the group of letters. Words can be found horizontally, vertically, or diagonally. They may read either forward or backward.

"When Dr. Roylott was in INDIA he MARRIED my mother, Mrs. Stoner, the YOUNG WIDOW of Major-General Stoner, of the BENGAL ARTILLERY. My sister JULIA and I were twins, and we were only two years old at the time of my mother's re-marriage. She had a CONSIDERABLE SUM of money—not less than £1000 a year—and this she BEQUEATHED to Dr. Roylott ENTIRELY while we RESIDED with him, with a PROVISION that a certain ANNUAL sum should be allowed to each of us in the event of our marriage. Shortly after our return to England my mother died—she was KILLED eight years ago in a RAILWAY ACCIDENT near CREWE. Dr. Roylott then ABANDONED his attempts to ESTABLISH himself in practice in London and took us to live with him in the old ANCESTRAL house at STOKE MORAN. The money which my mother had left was enough for ALL OUR WANTS, and there seemed to be NO OBSTACLE to our HAPPINESS."

```
D D N A Q P X J D K Y T N P W X J
E E Y V N S K E E C H O I S H P J
I L F R D C N A P R O V I S I O N
R L N W E O E R Y B C R E W E X A
A I K A D L E S S Y L E R I T N E
A K V N R S L T T Z L Y Q X N U D
M U A C I O A I P R C Q L U F D I
I B M D C C M C T X A P A Q D N P
A L E K L T Y E A R G L I I D T U
J D I E H E Y J K M A W D I L L T
Z L S T N A W R U O L L A L K U Z
E S T A B L I S H B T L A P E V J
Y O U N G W I D O W S S O G O F O
S S E N I P P A H K X G E D N J C
B E Q U E A T H E D D V I D N E S
C O N S I D E R A B L E S U M E B
R A I L W A Y A C C I D E N T P B
```

Answers on page 377.

The Adventure of the Speckled Band Story Pt. 4

Each word or phrase in all capitals in the Sherlock Holmes quotation below is contained within the group of letters. Words can be found horizontally, vertically, or diagonally. They may read either forward or backward.

"But a TERRIBLE CHANGE came over our stepfather about this time. Instead of MAKING FRIENDS and EXCHANGING VISITS with our NEIGHBOURS, who had at first been OVERJOYED to see a ROY-LOTT of Stoke Moran back in the OLD FAMILY SEAT, he shut himself up in his house and SELDOM came out save to INDULGE in FERO-CIOUS QUARRELS with whoever might CROSS HIS PATH. Violence of TEMPER approaching to MANIA has been HEREDITARY in the men of the family, and in my stepfather's case it had, I believe, been INTENSIFIED by his LONG RESIDENCE in the TROPICS. A series of DISGRACEFUL BRAWLS took place, two of which ended in the PO-LICE-COURT, until at last he became the TERROR OF THE VILLAGE, and the folks would fly at his approach, for he is a man of IMMENSE STRENGTH, and absolutely UNCONTROLLABLE in his ANGER.

```
F E R O C I O U S Q U A R R E L S Y W M F
Y R A T I D E R E H G W E S A N G E R D A
T E R R O R O F T H E V I L L A G E E I U
V C L E H T C R O S S H I S P A T H X S G
V L O N G R E S I D E N C E U V E E C G U
D O X E Q N L P T M C X D N R H U I H R V
K E U T X G A A L J A F E J I W W N A A X
W W I F S D V H W Q H Q M V G V S D N C C
T U Z F M P B C C T T O L Y O R V F G E U
Z F V I I I O R Q E K K G T X X L D I F C
G N Z L H S E L B A L L O R T N O C N U X
T M L A M O N W I S F B E X N N S L G L Q
O V E R J O Y E D C P B I R X C F R V B T
D N S M E Z D X T O E X F R I O A E I R I
Z D M A N I A L Y N D C A P R C A P S A N
K H W P M R W E E G I O O R C E T M I W D
U U W Q T J D R N S A R Z U X F T E T L U
N E I G H B O U R S T P N D R S H T S S L
O L D F A M I L Y S E A T T L T O C L V G
C G I M M E N S E S T R E N G T H P G E
M A K I N G F R I E N D S S R U J E T O C
```

Answers on page 377.

The Adventure of the Speckled Band Story Pt. 5

Each word or phrase in all capitals in the Sherlock Holmes quotation below is contained within the group of letters. Words can be found horizontally, vertically, or diagonally. They may read either forward or backward.

"You can IMAGINE from what I say that my POOR SISTER Julia and I had NO GREAT PLEASURE in our lives. No SERVANT would stay with us, and for a LONG TIME we did all the WORK OF THE HOUSE. She was but THIRTY at the time of her death, and yet her hair had already begun to WHITEN, even as mine has…She died just TWO YEARS AGO, and it is of her death that I WISH TO SPEAK to you. You can understand that, living the life which I have described, we were LITTLE LIKELY to see anyone of our own AGE AND POSITION. We had, however, an aunt, my mother's MAIDEN sister, Miss Honoria WESTPHAIL, who lives near HARROW, and we were OCCASIONALLY allowed to pay SHORT VISITS at this lady's house. Julia went there at CHRISTMAS two years ago, and met there a half-pay MAJOR OF MARINES, to whom she became engaged. My stepfather learned of the engagement when my sister returned and offered NO OBJECTION to the marriage; but within a FORTNIGHT of the day which had been fixed for the wedding, the TERRIBLE EVENT occurred which has DEPRIVED me of my only COMPANION."

```
W J B M N G A Y W E A O P H A R R O W
A L F A O W O R K O F T H E H O U S E
L N Y J G E S M O C Q R M A I D E N N
G N L O R W I S H T O S P E A K R K I
Y N L R E M Q O R X D M W A X D V P G
Z O A O A N O I T I S O P D N A E G A
L I N F T Q J Y U X A W T A F Q U M M
O T O M P D E P R I V E D A N L B Y I
N C I A L T E S H O R T V I S I T S V
G E S R E T S I S R O O P N F W O H R
T J A I A E W L I T L D A X E V V N E
I B C N S Y Z B Z I V H N F O T R Z T
M O C E U Q L H O E L H A A R K I N Y
E O O S R E G X C E Q Y U K I N A H E
C N B T E E S A M T S I R H C V U E W
Q T K V N I L T T H G I N T R O F Q L
C Z E N L I T T L E L I K E L Y M N S
U N G Y T R I H T T W E S T P H A I L
T W O Y E A R S A G O N I L S J A J I
```

Answers on page 377.

The Adventure of the Speckled Band Death Pt. 1

Each word or phrase in all capitals in the Sherlock Holmes quotation below is contained within the group of letters. Words can be found horizontally, vertically, or diagonally. They may read either forward or backward.

"I could NOT SLEEP that night. A VAGUE FEELING of impending MISFORTUNE impressed me. My sister and I, you will RECOLLECT, were twins, and you know how SUBTLE are the links which BIND TWO SOULS which are so CLOSELY ALLIED. It was a WILD NIGHT. The wind was howling outside, and the rain was BEATING and SPLASHING against the windows. Suddenly, amid all the HUBBUB of the gale, there BURST FORTH the WILD SCREAM of a TERRIFIED WOMAN. I knew that it was my sister's voice. I sprang from my bed, wrapped a SHAWL round me, and rushed into the CORRIDOR. As I opened my door I seemed to hear a LOW WHISTLE, such as my sister described, and a few MOMENTS later a CLANGING sound, as if a MASS OF METAL had fallen."

```
T C L O S E L Y A L L I E D R F I
H S N V Q B N H Q C K G J S A R A
G L H I V A G U E F E E L I N G K
I U T R L E V B C U W D T B H W Y
N O P O A R N B U R S T F O R T H
D S Z D T W U U E L T B U S S N Q
L O R I E J V B T E U R B G T O C
I W E R M K J I S R W Z N H N T G
W T C R F Q Y N X V O I Z S E S G
M D O O R Z D H B H F H A M L N
U N L C S S J C Z S E A S S O E I
W I L D S C R E A M W A C I M E G
J B E W A V N L C L Q D T Y M P N
N S C F M X P B H I U V R I S M A
D E T E D S T G A K K P X Y N R L
U T E R R I F I E D W O M A N G C
L O W W H I S T L E M G P E A Z D
```

Answers on page 377.

The Adventure of the Speckled Band Death Pt. 2

Each word or phrase in all capitals in the Sherlock Holmes quotation below is contained within the group of letters. Words can be found horizontally, vertically, or diagonally. They may read either forward or backward.

As I ran down the PASSAGE, my sister's door was UNLOCKED, and REVOLVED SLOWLY upon its HINGES. I stared at it HORROR-STRICKEN, not knowing what was about to ISSUE from it. By the light of the CORRIDOR-LAMP I saw my sister APPEAR at the OPENING, her face BLANCHED with TERROR, her hands GROPING for help, her whole figure SWAYING to and fro like that of a DRUNKARD. I ran to her and threw my arms round her, but at that moment her KNEES seemed to GIVE WAY and she fell to the ground. She WRITHED as one who is in TERRIBLE PAIN, and her LIMBS were DREADFULLY CONVULSED.

```
N S E G N I H Q X S C Y N K I Z W N D
I S A U A R R Y L R Q A K H Q D B E E
A X P A S S A G E O V W I D F E W K S
P Z A I X S Q N W R M E H G F H N C L
E D L X L L I W R R F V K N Y C Y I U
L L I M B S E Y I E I I L L Q N Q R V
B D K P Z K R X T T H G W L C A Q T N
I F P U J W D S H M Q O R D H L N S O
R W P G D I G Y E U L E J O U B S R C
R X X W K C Z R D S T I C C Q W G O Y
E N P M A L R O D I R R O C A R S R L
T D M J U B O E L T U B P Y O T F R L
I R X Y N D V I O J Q A I P G C M O U
N A A Y L L I B W R A N I G N B H H F
S K R I O R B N E P G N S N I Z S N D
T N Y V C X L G P P G H K O N F K S A
F U E V K S E E N K H K S P E G M A E
R R Q A E C A E A Q U S O A P Z B A R
F D E J D R Y H Z B P G V P O J K B D
```

Answers on page 378.

The Adventure of the Speckled Band Death Pt. 3

Each word or phrase in all capitals in the Sherlock Holmes quotation below is contained within the group of letters. Words can be found horizontally, vertically, or diagonally. They may read either forward or backward.

"At first I thought that she had not RECOGNISED me, but as I bent over her she SUDDENLY SHRIEKED out in a voice which I shall NEVER FORGET, 'Oh, my God! HELEN! It was the band! The SPECKLED BAND!' There was something else which she would FAIN HAVE SAID, and she STABBED with her FINGER into the air in the direction of the DOCTOR'S ROOM, but a FRESH CONVULSION seized her and CHOKED HER WORDS. I rushed out, CALLING LOUDLY for my stepfather, and I met him HASTENING from his room in his DRESSING-GOWN. When he reached my sister's side she was UNCONSCIOUS, and though he POURED BRANDY down her THROAT and sent for MEDICAL AID from the VILLAGE, all efforts were in vain, for she SLOWLY SANK and died without having RECOVERED her consciousness. Such was the DREADFUL END of my BELOVED SISTER."

```
Y B N M W A X N D V D Y D M A M E M D S K
A Z G Y R U G R E O C H U V B X F I S V N
R T K V X E O Q C V C R R H X U A P U A A
B S S G B R T T D R E A D F U L E N D S S
V P B U K N O S E H P R S E A P D Y D C Y
C C O A O R C C I M A P F C T I E V E M L
N R X U S I O U C S E S I O A G F R N I W
E E X R R G C Q D C D D T S R N K G L S O
V C O U N E R S K J E E E E W G R F Y F L
R O S I C I D L N M A V V O N I E N S I S
M V S U O X E B U O A T G O V I X T H N A
M E N Q J D E X R H C G H Z L D N W R G R
D R B E B S U G N A N N E R X E E G I E D
S E G A L Z E I A I N M U K O W B L E R F
T D N R A E A G S L C D U I Y A Y N K N N
A D A X V F H S D M L U Y M N P T S E B P
B I K D J D E A B Q J I I F G W Z M D M E
B W P T N R N O I S L U V N O C H S E R F
E I U R D C A L L I N G L O U D L Y B K T
D Q F O S D R O W R E H D E K O H C R R Q
J J B A P I A U K D W G U B O P C K L X B
```

 Answers on page 378.

The Adventure of the Engineer's Thumb

Every word listed is contained within the group of letters. Words can be found in a straight line horizontally, vertically, or diagonally. They may be read either forward or backward.

CLEAVER	HYSTERICAL
COUNTERFEIT	LYSANDER STARK
DR. BECHER	MURDEROUS
ENGINEER	NERVES
EYFORD	PALE
FERGUSON	THUMB
FULLERS EARTH	TWEED
HORSE	VICTOR HATHERLEY
HYDRAULIC	

```
F S U O R E D R U M U L T Z L
R E E N I G N E K C P A I X K
B M U H T W X Y M I U C E B R
E K F S Y C P F A L P I F N A
K M X U Q A G O D U A R R O T
G G A G L A B R P A L E E S S
E S R O H L B D B R E T T U R
W S P T W E E D R D D S N G E
N P Z T C B S R Q Y L Y U R D
C H B H Z U R E S H N H O E N
T V E F Y E T L V E U X C F A
Y R P I V S A R F R A H Z C S
V I C T O R H A T H E R L E Y
V W Z D V X J O A O C N T D L
R E V A E L C T D W R Z T H P
```

Answers on page 378.

The Adventure of
the Engineer's Thumb Passage 1

Each word or phrase in all capitals in the Sherlock Holmes quotation below is contained within the group of letters. Words can be found horizontally, vertically, or diagonally. They may read either forward or backward.

"I shall HAVE TO TELL my tale to the POLICE; but, between OURSELVES, if it were not for the CONVINCING EVIDENCE of this WOUND OF MINE, I should be SURPRISED if they BELIEVED my STATEMENT, for it is a very EXTRAORDINARY one, and I have not much in the WAY OF PROOF with which to BACK IT UP; and, even if they believe me, the CLUES which I can give them are so VAGUE that it is a QUESTION whether JUSTICE will be done."

```
X S C T Y X A P O F G N C J X Y V O Q
L A A P E Z U P H W Y O B I V A G U E
Q H X C B T U J F O W F D R V X H L Q
H Q I Y I C W H A V E T O T E L L U W
D T X K R T X Q I E B O Z J P W B O O
F L C R S A N P L G U E T V A S I K U
L A J G P S N K R R F R L Y P O B Y N
B M S U R P R I S E D Y O I T Y W V D
X L P V J I Q E D G V F D L E V N H O
T N B Y I E L Q T R P A I N E V F J F
H V R P C V U K Z R O W B C L U E S M
T W Q I E E M E O D N A Y X U C D D I
M W L S S E I O Q K R C R Q I Y V C N
B O W T S T F W J Q H I R T Z O C Z E
P H I C K R Y A L Q T O S G X F Z M N
T O R Q D O K F O L U U R Q K E O K K
N J Y O H M R H Y X J H B N V K D Y D
C O N V I N C I N G E V I D E N C E S
L R X H T N E M E T A T S E C Y U O
```

Answers on page 378.

The Adventure of the Engineer's Thumb Passage 2

Each word or phrase in all capitals in the Sherlock Holmes quotation below is contained within the group of letters. Words can be found horizontally, vertically, or diagonally. They may read either forward or backward.

The story has, I believe, been told MORE THAN ONCE in the NEWSPAPERS, but, like all such NARRATIVES, its effect is much LESS STRIKING when set forth EN BLOCIN a single HALF-COLUMN of PRINT than when the facts SLOWLY EVOLVE before your OWN EYES, and the mystery CLEARS GRADUALLY away as each NEW DISCOVERY furnishes a step which leads on to the COMPLETE TRUTH. At the time the CIRCUMSTANCES made a DEEP IMPRESSION upon me, and the LAPSE of two years has HARDLY SERVED to WEAKEN the EFFECT.

```
J C L M H L H N L E S P A L H K C
V W E D E E P I M P R E S S I O N
V E S X S W H J B I D E A L B E M
N A S R R L A A N N Y Y O J C F K
E K S C H V O T L E A S Y N J G E
W E T I E C V W N F E D O X Q J B
D N R R Q F G W L V C N S M B B I
I E I C M C O X I Y A O H I N I N
S F K U N H M T V H E A L J E M E
C F I M A C A C T P S V C U J G W
O E N S C R N E E I G Z O F M M S
V C G T R E R N V G M Z E L P N P
E T P A M O D N B Y M A I C V H A
R F N N M W E N B L O C I N G E P
Y C E C O M P L E T E T R U T H E
O C L E A R S G R A D U A L L Y R
S F E S H A R D L Y S E R V E D S
```

Answers on page 379.

The Adventure of the Engineer's Thumb Passage 3

Each word or phrase in all capitals in the Sherlock Holmes quotation below is contained within the group of letters. Words can be found horizontally, vertically, or diagonally. They may read either forward or backward.

" 'We are now,' said he, 'ACTUALLY within the HYDRAULIC PRESS, and it would be a particularly UNPLEASANT thing for us if ANYONE were to turn it on. The CEILING of this SMALL CHAMBER is really the end of the DESCENDING PISTON, and it COMES DOWN with the FORCE of MANY TONS upon this METAL FLOOR. There are small LATERAL COLUMNS of WATER outside which RECEIVE the force, and which TRANSMIT and MULTIPLY it in the manner which is FAMILIAR to you. The MACHINE goes READILY enough, but there is some STIFFNESS in the working of it, and it has lost a little of its force. PERHAPS you will have the GOODNESS to look it over and to show us how we can SET IT RIGHT.'"

```
S X Y R Z J R B H U S M J E J Q O Y S
K P V B E I B T V P I A D N G Y R S N
M V X L L C K A U Q D E O C R O E M
E C R O F O E H E R A Q O Y A E O T U
G M S W E M R I A M D D P N M B L I L
A Q S T M E F M V H N Q R A I M F T O
K S E N P S X P D E N A N Z E A L R C
O R R A I D C Y S Q I Y Y N D H A I L
G Q P S Q O G S H L T S I X T C T G A
U N C A Y W G H I O T H A M A L E H R
Y Q I E B N D M N I C E C V J L M T E
H H L L A D A S F A U T T U V A Q F T
T Y U P I F L F M Y R Y U B O M S W A
V E A N R E N P O A Z F A X U S P Z L
D S R U I E C U N E Q M L V U H N X O
L W D Z S V T S C I B Y L P I T L U M
F N Y S N T M A N U G C Y J T D T Y E
W U H O B I H U W Y L I D A E R S C Q
J D N O T S I P G N I D N E C S E D Q
```

Answers on page 379.

Telephone Records

A local artist named George Wilson has been reported missing. The police have learned that five calls were made from his cell phone on the night he disappeared. None of the five calls were to the same number, and each of them lasted for a different length of time. Using only the clues below, help sort out the information by matching each call to its owner, number, and time, and determine the length of each phone call.

1. Mitchell's phone number doesn't start with "368".

2. The longest phone call was placed five minutes before George dialed 731-9262, and sometime before he called Sarah.

3. Charlie's number is 447-6995.

4. The 48-second phone call was to either Kerry or whoever has the phone number starting with "731".

5. George dialed 592-0021 15 minutes after the 22-second phone call.

6. Whoever received the 3-minute phone call, the person George called at 2:07am, and Vicky are three different people.

7. George called Vicky sometime before 2:10am.

8. Of the two calls placed before 2:00am, one lasted for 3 minutes and the other was to the "239" number.

9. Kerry's home phone number is 239-4827.

10. The 2:07am call didn't last for exactly a minute and a half.

	People					Numbers					Lengths				
	Charlie	Kerry	Mitchell	Sarah	Vicky	239-4827	368-7841	447-6995	592-0021	731-9262	22 seconds	35 seconds	48 seconds	1.5 minutes	3 minutes
Times 1:52am															
1:57am															
2:02am															
2:07am															
2:12am															
Lengths 22 seconds															
35 seconds															
48 seconds															
1.5 minutes															
3 minutes															
Numbers 239-4827															
368-7841															
447-6995															
592-0021															
731-9262															

Times	People	Numbers	Lengths
1:52am			
1:57am			
2:02am			
2:07am			
2:12am			

Answers on page 379.

The Adventure of the Noble Bachelor

Every word listed is contained within the group of letters. Words can be found in a straight line horizontally, vertically, or diagonally. They may be read either forward or backward.

ALICE	LORD ST SIMON
BALMORAL	MINING
BREAKFAST	MORNING POST
DOWRY	PLANTAGENET
DUKE	SAN FRANCISCO
FLORA MILLAR	SERPENTINE
GROSVENOR MANSIONS	TUDOR
HATTY DORAN	VANISHING
LOCKET	WEDDING

```
S T A J T H S M M U M Q H M T J B
N X S Y B U I M G J L A G E A P F
O P F A L D D O C D L M N R L J Y
I K S Z F C R O Y A Z E Y Y K X K
S M W A F K Z A R K G N J M H H G
N W T J N Y A O Z A T I B H O A Z
A Q O N R F M E T M S T I N W T L
M P W W K L R N R H O N V W O T O
R Z O G A B A A U B P E P G S Y R
O D A B N L S W N L G P K M P D D
N I L A P I L L B C N R I U Y O S
E L I R Y U D E Y K I E L M D R T
V O C Y G B C D D E N S T C X A S
S C E T R R L W E A R O C Q N N I
O K M G N I N I M W O X E O D C M
R E S K J F L O R A M I L L A R O
G T S V O A V A N I S H I N G D N
```

 Answers on page 379.

The Adventure of the Noble Bachelor Letter

Each word or phrase in all capitals in the Sherlock Holmes quotation below is contained within the group of letters. Words can be found horizontally, vertically, or diagonally. They may read either forward or backward.

My DEAR Mr. Sherlock Holmes:—Lord Backwater tells me that I may place IMPLICIT RELIANCE upon your JUDGMENT and DISCRETION. I have DETERMINED, therefore, to CALL UPON YOU and to CONSULT you in REFERENCE to the very PAINFUL EVENT which has OCCURRED in CONNECTION with my WEDDING. Mr. Lestrade, of SCOTLAND YARD, is acting already in the MATTER, but he ASSURES me that he sees NO OBJECTION to your co-operation, and that he even thinks that it might be of some assistance. I will call at FOUR O'CLOCK in the AFTERNOON, and, should you have any other ENGAGEMENT at that time, I hope that you will POSTPONE it, as this matter is of PARAMOUNT importance. Yours FAITHFULLY, St. Simon.

```
I M P L I C I T R E L I A N C E G
K K J J P M H D J R T M J K V N U
R T N U O M A R A P A W Y M I E P
E E N M D C L A U T X E H D N F P
F N O N U G O T T R B D O M Q P
E O I O O N M E N L S E R U S S A
R P T I Y O R E R E W V O R Z K I
E T E T N O D E N I M R E T E D N
N S R C O N S U L T D E M M M K F
C O C E P R M E P I E M G W F T U
E P S J U E V L C O R Z K A L R L
N A I B L T J V G A R S V F G I E
L H D O L F A I T F U L L Y F N V
O G Q O A A S N D D C Y V V I F E
K Z E N C F O U R O C L O C K I N
E D R A Y D N A L T O C S U N C T
V Z E Z C S C O N N E C T I O N V
```

Answers on page 379.

The Adventure of the Noble Bachelor Article Pt. 1

Each word or phrase in all capitals in the Sherlock Holmes quotation below is contained within the group of letters. Words can be found horizontally, vertically, or diagonally. They may read either forward or backward.

The FAMILY of Lord Robert St. Simon has been THROWN into the greatest CONSTERNATION by the STRANGE AND PAINFUL episodes which have taken place in CONNECTION with his wedding. The CEREMONY, as shortly ANNOUNCED in the PAPERS of YESTERDAY, occurred on the PREVIOUS MORNING; but it is only now that it has been POSSIBLE to CONFIRM the strange RUMOURS which have been so PERSISTENTLY floating about. In spite of the attempts of the friends to hush the matter up, so much public attention has now been DRAWN to it that no GOOD PURPOSE can be served by AFFECTING to DISREGARD what is a COMMON subject for CONVERSATION.

```
S T R A N G E A N D P A I N F U L M J
N D I S R E G A R D P X M T C F J O E
X W N Y X L H A F F D C O N F I R M
N B O P Y L I M A F V M X E Y X C U D
O Y F R R M W W B H E C Q X Q E E M Y
I E V S H E V D M M F C Y T I A R O A
T L J R V T V F C B G T T X Z Q E U D
A V C E C B P I S O V M E I S S M R R
N Z Q P O P R J O C R L B W N Y O S E
R T J A N Q J D T U B N C F P G N F T
E W L P V B P I E I S O W L U C Y N S
T Y W G E U J N S O N M H A H O O V E
S H M E R W T S D N P E O H R M J D Y
N J P P S M O E E K J S J R M D O O G
O A O L A P T C D E C N U O N N A J A
C S S Z T K T B M J W L C B Z I P M C
E T T A I I Y N Q U D X C Z H E N W P
U E Z R O T S T G X P E Z J N P H G C
J T I N N Y L T N E T S I S R E P Y Z
```

Answers on page 380.

The Adventure of the Noble Bachelor Article Pt. 2

Each word or phrase in all capitals in the Sherlock Holmes quotation below is contained within the group of letters. Words can be found horizontally, vertically, or diagonally. They may read either forward or backward.

'The CEREMONY, which was PERFORMED at St. George's, HANOVER SQUARE, was a VERY QUIET one, no one being present save the FATHER OF THE BRIDE, Mr. Aloysius Doran, the DUCHESS OF BALMORAL, Lord Backwater, Lord Eustace and Lady Clara St. Simon (the YOUNGER BROTHER and sister of the BRIDEGROOM), and Lady Alicia Whittington. The WHOLE PARTY proceeded AFTERWARDS to the house of Mr. Aloysius Doran, at Lancaster Gate, where BREAKFAST had been PREPARED. It appears that some LITTLE TROUBLE was caused by a woman, whose name has not been ASCERTAINED, who ENDEAVOURED to force her way into the house after the BRIDAL PARTY, alleging that she had SOME CLAIM upon Lord St. Simon. It was only after a PAINFUL AND PROLONGED scene that she was EJECTED by the BUTLER and the FOOTMAN.

```
E R A U Q S R E V O N A H Q M V T N Y
W R E H T O R B R E G N U O Y E M P T
C L K P C E R E M O N Y O N S R U X R
A I M I A L C E M O S R A N G Y Z H A
I T D W M Z T W W S G M D H Y Q A A P
Z T D S D R A W R E T F A F T U T Y E
B L E J D X K D D O C Y P J R I J F L
R E R E I G T I O T R E T P A E D F O
E T O P F I R F B M R I A K P T E Y H
A R V R I B D U E F U V D X L F R W W
K O A B P G T E O I Y Q H M A B A L D
F U E Y M L R R T F D Q X P D K P V X
A B D T E D M A S C E R T A I N E D K
S L N R G E D S I F E G T K R U R K R
T E E W D Z O Y E P I J W T B R P G P
L A R O M L A B F O S S E H C U D W T
F A T H E R O F T H E B R I D E K F O
P A I N F U L A N D P R O L O N G E D
X B G S E Q D U R D U Q U H F G H T D
```

Answers on page 380.

The Adventure of the Noble Bachelor Article Pt. 3

Each word or phrase in all capitals in the Sherlock Holmes quotation below is contained within the group of letters. Words can be found horizontally, vertically, or diagonally. They may read either forward or backward.

The BRIDE, who had FORTUNATELY entered the HOUSE before this unpleasant INTERRUPTION, had sat down to BREAKFAST with the rest, when she COMPLAINED of a sudden INDISPOSITION and RETIRED to her room. Her PROLONGED ABSENCE having caused SOME COMMENT, her father FOLLOWED her, but learned from her MAID that she had only come up to her CHAMBER for an instant, caught up an ULSTER AND BONNET, and HURRIED down to the PASSAGE. One of the FOOTMEN declared that he had seen a lady leave the house thus APPARELLED, but had REFUSED to credit that it was his MISTRESS, believing her to be with the COMPANY.

```
H  F  U  L  S  T  E  R  A  N  D  B  O  N  N  E  T
Y  L  E  T  A  N  U  T  R  O  F  C  M  H  O  E  F
D  M  Y  L  N  L  Q  K  G  O  F  C  U  W  I  C  E
A  I  I  S  O  X  W  R  V  M  H  R  B  U  T  N  M
S  R  A  S  I  C  B  V  J  A  R  B  I  P  P  E  Y
O  N  E  M  T  O  O  F  M  I  D  K  V  P  U  S  E
M  O  A  N  I  R  M  B  E  N  E  D  E  D  R  B  G
E  Y  I  F  S  D  E  D  Y  G  W  Y  E  E  R  A  A
C  N  Q  C  O  R  D  S  I  Z  O  L  E  N  E  D  S
O  A  Q  T  P  G  E  E  S  C  L  I  M  I  T  E  S
M  P  J  D  S  Q  H  U  S  E  L  Y  U  A  N  G  A
M  M  T  G  I  N  X  O  R  U  O  O  T  L  I  N  P
E  O  E  X  D  H  X  A  U  E  F  D  A  P  J  O  I
N  C  M  P  N  G  P  M  Q  S  D  E  D  M  H  L  F
T  T  J  F  I  P  O  P  W  N  E  I  R  O  D  O  U
S  T  T  S  A  F  K  A  E  R  B  Z  R  C  D  R  J
H  Y  K  Q  W  R  E  T  I  R  E  D  P  B  E  P  G
```

Answers on page 380.

The Adventure of
the Noble Bachelor Article Pt. 4

Each word or phrase in all capitals in the Sherlock Holmes quotation below is contained within the group of letters. Words can be found horizontally, vertically, or diagonally. They may read either forward or backward.

On ASCERTAINING that his DAUGHTER had disappeared, Mr. Aloysius Doran, in CONJUNCTION with the BRIDEGROOM, instantly put themselves in COMMUNICATION with the police, and very ENERGETIC inquiries are being made, which will probably RESULT in a SPEEDY CLEARING UP of this very SINGULAR BUSINESS. Up to a LATE HOUR last night, however, nothing had TRANSPIRED as to the WHEREABOUTS of the MISSING LADY. There are rumours of FOUL PLAY in the matter, and it is said that the police have caused the ARREST of the woman who had caused the original DISTURBANCE, in the belief that, from JEALOUSY or some other MOTIVE, she may have been CONCERNED in the strange DISAPPEARANCE of the bride.

```
S S E N I S U B R A L U G N I S E
W P L C E I F K W V G X S T R L T
G U A C O V U K P V X M C S J S L
X G S K H M I Y S U O L A E J P U
E N C Y W K M T T D T I O R B W S
H I E A H Y D U O P V K D R R D E
N R R L E L Y S N M U Y A A I I R
C A T P R F A V I I E B U K D S T
O E A L E C J T W N C F G Q E T R
N L I U A U T I E G Y A H I G U A
C C N O B D R R P H U D T R R R N
E Y I F O P G N Y Z O Q E I O B S
R D N I U E J F B B U U R X O A P
N E G Q T U H U L Y Y J R V M N I
E E D I S A P P E A R A N C E C R
D P C O N J U N C T I O N P A E E
C S M I S S I N G L A D Y T J Y D
```

Answers on page 380.

Smuggled Electronics

The F.B.I. has received a tip-off that a notorious criminal gang is planning to smuggle counterfeit electronics out of Amity Airport this morning. The informant indicated that 5 different shipments (each containing a different type of consumer electronic device) would go out, each on a different flight. Help the agents bust this smuggling ring by matching each illegal shipment to its flight number, departure time, and gate number.

1. The cell phones are going out of either gate 6 or gate 11.

2. The flight at gate 18 will leave 7 minutes before the one out of gate 3.

3. The earliest departure isn't at gate 7.

4. Flight 92 is either the one with the laptops or the one leaving at 8:17am.

5. Flight 233 will depart sometime after 8:05am.

6. The plane that departs at 8:24am, the one with the counterfeit tablets, and the one leaving from gate 11 are three different flights.

7. Of the tablet and the laptop shipments, one will leave at 8:31am and the other is stored on flight 356.

8. Of the plane at gate 3 and Flight 233, one has a shipment of flat-screen televisions and the other will depart at 8:17am.

9. The watch shipment is scheduled to depart sometime before the plane with the illegal cell phones (which isn't flight 108).

10. Flight 356 will leave 7 minutes after the plane at gate 18.

	Flights					Gates					Items				
	92	108	233	356	510	3	6	7	11	18	Cell phones	Laptops	Tablets	Televisions	Watches
Departures 8:03am															
8:10am															
8:17am															
8:24am															
8:31am															
Items Cell phones															
Laptops															
Tablets															
Televisions															
Watches															
Gates 3															
6															
7															
11															
18															

Departures	Flights	Gates	Items
8:03am			
8:10am			
8:17am			
8:24am			
8:31am			

313   *Answers on page 381.*

The Adventure of Black Peter

Each word or phrase in all capitals in the Sherlock Holmes quotation below is contained within the group of letters. Words can be found horizontally, vertically, or diagonally. They may read either forward or backward.

I have never known my friend to be in BETTER form, both mental and physical, than in the year '95. His increasing FAME had brought with it an IMMENSE practice, and I should be guilty of an INDISCRETION if I were even to hint at the identity of some of the ILLUSTRIOUS clients who crossed our humble THRESHOLD in Baker Street. Holmes, however, like all great ARTISTS, lived for his art's sake, and, save in the case of the Duke of Holdernesse, I have seldom known him claim any large REWARD for his INESTIMABLE services. So UNWORLDLY was he—or so CAPRICIOUS—that he frequently REFUSED his help to the powerful and WEALTHY where the problem made no APPEAL to his sympathies, while he would devote weeks of most INTENSE application to the AFFAIRS of some humble client whose case presented those strange and DRAMATIC qualities which appealed to his imagination and CHALLENGED his INGENUITY.

```
W S O Y D R A M A T I C Y K N
K C U Y T I U N E G N I A V O
N D N O W A D U M B V N F Y I
V U B S I C P E Q P W T F H T
D N G Q U C U P S K Q E A T E
E W R A A O I J E U Q N I L R
G O E A R M I R R A F S R A C
N R T R T K E R P O L E S E S
E L T E I E M R T A M Y R W I
L D E W S S A Z S S C S I R D
L L B A T N F O J M U S L I N
A Y U R S E L S Z J L L S L I
H T J D D M Z M I K S Y L U P
C E L B A M I T S E N I N I V
Y N B D H I T H R E S H O L D
```

Answers on page 381.

Crack the Password

A detective has found a memory aid that the criminal left behind, a list of coded passwords. The detective knows that the criminal likes to scramble each password, then remove the same letter from each word. Can you figure out the missing letter and unscramble each word in this set to reveal the passwords?

SINE

PRIMERS

LEARN

MICAS

Crack the Password

A detective has found a memory aid that the criminal left behind, a list of coded passwords. The detective knows that the criminal likes to scramble each password, then remove the same letter from each word. Can you figure out the missing letter and unscramble each word in this set to reveal the passwords?

AROMA

TRANCE

FOAMING

AMICUS

Answers on page 381.

The Adventure of the Beryl Coronet Letter

Each word or phrase in all capitals in the Sherlock Holmes quotation below is contained within the group of letters. Words can be found horizontally, vertically, or diagonally. They may read either forward or backward.

My DEAREST UNCLE:–I feel that I have brought TROUBLE UPON YOU, and that if I had acted DIFFERENTLY this terrible MISFORTUNE might never have OCCURRED. I cannot, with this THOUGHT in my MIND, ever again be HAPPY under your ROOF, and I feel that I must leave you FOREVER. Do not worry about my FUTURE, for that is provided for; and, above all, do not search for me, for it will be FRUITLESS LABOUR and an ILL-SERVICE to me. In life or IN DEATH, I am ever your LOVING.

MARY.

```
O C C U R R E D C G P E R K K
D M L T F R A C X P D P U U U
I U O Y N O P U E L B U O R T
F Q Z M Y J Y E D O S K B I M
F B L E L C N U T S E R A E D
E K H A P P Y H R E G J L H E
R V L B H D O H M N F E S R C
E N V F N U F T L U O L S E I
N L V I G L C A E T O B E V V
T O M H R I R E W R R I L E R
L V T G M R X D K O U G T R E
Y I L Y F U E N B F C T I O S
N N T R V X J I W S O R U F L
V G T A O Z W N C I D W R F L
S T W M T Q A T T M Y W F W I
```

319   *Answers on page 381.*

The Adventure of the Beryl Coronet Passage 1

Each word or phrase in all capitals in the Sherlock Holmes quotation below is contained within the group of letters. Words can be found horizontally, vertically, or diagonally. They may read either forward or backward.

"It is UNFORTUNATELY more than POSSIBLE; it is CERTAIN. Neither you nor YOUR SON knew the TRUE CHARACTER of this man when you ADMITTED him into your FAMILY CIRCLE. He is one of the most DANGEROUS men in England—a RUINED GAMBLER, an absolutely DESPERATE VILLAIN, a man without HEART or CONSCIENCE. Your NIECE knew nothing of such men. When he BREATHED his vows to her, as he had done to A HUNDRED BEFORE her, she FLATTERED herself that she alone had TOUCHED his heart. The DEVIL KNOWS BEST what he said, but at least she became his TOOL and was in the HABIT of seeing him nearly EVERY EVENING."

```
G Y D H Y L E T A N U T R O F N U
N Q O E O Y J R I F N I T C E I T
I L C U H E A Y L V O R D K R A T
N O H O R C K M J X A T D Q O L X
E O B O N S U S S E W R S C F L G
V T U U Q S O O H Y P K U E E I A
E C E I N J C N T O S B O R B V D
Y F W K N A N I S J S O R T D E M
R L M M I H Y S E B G A E A E T I
E A P U I A I K S N R L G I R A T
V T V N X B B T Z B C E N N D R T
E T W W L I O F G V Z E A K N E E
P E A E Q T S Y Z E K H D T U P D
N R U I N E D G A M B L E R H S K
D E V I L K N O W S B E S T A E Q
K D F A M I L Y C I R C L E X D D
Y K D R E T C A R A H C E U R T U
```

Answers on page 381.

Grave Robberies

The state police have been called in to investigate a series of bizarre grave robberies perpetrated in five different cemeteries across Bolton County. Each occurred on a different date and at a different cemetery, none of which were in the same town. Only one grave was robbed in each cemetery. Using only the clues below, help the police solve this mystery by determining the date on which each of the five graves were robbed, as well as the cemetery and town in which each was located.

1. Of the March 20th incident and the one at Dinby Dale Cemetery, one was in Upperdale and the other involved the grave of Ed Lowder.

2. Pat Fowler was interred at Green Lawn Cemetery in Shell City.

3. Holden Bray's grave (which was in either Calvary Cape Cemetery or the cemetery in Verona) was robbed 8 days before the incident in Trenton.

4. Brad Beaudry's grave wasn't robbed on the night of March 20th.

5. Of the two robberies in Upperdale and Shell City, one was at Apple Pine Cemetery and the other was on March 28th.

6. Ed Lowder wasn't buried in Verona.

7. The cemetery in Upperdale was robbed sometime before the one in Wilmette.

	Cemeteries					Graves					Towns				
	Apple Pine	Box Grove	Calvary Cape	Dinby Dale	Green Lawn	Brad Beaudry	Ed Lowder	Holden Bray	Pat Fowler	Ruben Yates	Shell City	Trenton	Upperdale	Verona	Wilmette
Dates March 12th															
March 20th															
March 28th															
April 5th															
April 13th															
Towns Shell City															
Trenton															
Upperdale															
Verona															
Wilmette															
Graves Brad Beaudry															
Ed Lowder															
Holden Bray															
Pat Fowler															
Ruben Yates															

Dates	Cemeteries	Graves	Towns
March 12th			
March 20th			
March 28th			
April 5th			
April 13th			

323

Answers on page 381.

The Five Orange Pips

Every all capital word listed is contained within the group of letters. Words can be found in a straight line horizontally, vertically, or diagonally. They may be read either forward or backward.

ATTIC

BICYCLE FACTORY

CIVIL WAR

DUNDEE

ELIAS

HORSHAM

INDIA

JOHN OPENSHAW

JOSEPH

LONESTAR

ORANGE PIPS

PONDICHERRY

SUNDIAL

```
Q P E A Y X P R C C E H M N G
F P F I N X D A I V W Y M M L
Q R G D L T S W T H A H Q P P
O H B N Z B W L T A B G X P O
R O P I X B P I A S X E Z B N
A R E E N X V B I S W B Q D
N S E K S W U I D L D O M R I
G H D T R O Z C E S E N S A C
E A N K V O J L G G F K U T H
P M U B D H I S Z B C V H S E
I Q D W O A L O B P I K J E R
P W A H S N E P O N H O J N R
S J L Q B M M T I G B I Z O Y
X H U G B N M G V E G O V L D
B I C Y C L E F A C T O R Y U
```

Answers on page 382.

The Five Orange Pips Tragedy Pt. 1

Each word or phrase in all capitals in the Sherlock Holmes quotation below is contained within the group of letters. Words can be found horizontally, vertically, or diagonally. They may read either forward or backward.

Between NINE AND TEN last night Police-CONSTABLE COOK, of the H Division, on duty near WATERLOO BRIDGE, heard a CRY FOR HELP and a SPLASH in the WATER. The night, however, was extremely DARK AND STORMY, so that, in spite of the help of several PASSERSBY, it was quite IMPOSSIBLE to effect a RESCUE. The ALARM, however, was given, and, by the aid of the water-police, the body was eventually RECOVERED. It proved to be that of a young GENTLEMAN whose NAME, as it appears from an ENVELOPE which was found in his POCKET, was John Openshaw, and whose RESIDENCE is near HORSHAM.

```
E  C  O  N  S  T  A  B  L  E  C  O  O  K  R
Z  T  W  Q  J  Y  P  N  L  U  L  G  C  A  E
P  A  S  S  E  R  S  B  Y  C  E  E  W  G  H
D  P  E  V  X  X  W  M  C  S  G  F  D  G  C
E  L  G  W  E  B  E  C  N  E  D  I  S  E  R
R  E  I  F  X  T  O  Z  T  R  R  S  Q  N  I
E  H  W  W  A  T  E  R  O  B  H  P  P  T  M
V  R  D  R  H  P  K  K  O  H  K  L  V  L  P
O  O  N  A  J  C  E  O  C  S  S  A  O  E  O
C  F  A  C  T  P  L  G  W  O  E  S  L  M  S
E  Y  M  H  O  R  S  H  A  M  P  H  R  A  S
R  R  E  N  E  T  D  N  A  E  N  I  N  N  I
D  C  W  T  M  U  Q  G  Z  D  Z  L  U  Z  B
R  D  A  R  K  A  N  D  S  T  O  R  M  Y  L
P  W  M  R  A  L  A  E  N  V  E  L  O  P  E
```

 Answers on page 382.

The Five Orange Pips Tragedy Pt. 2

Each word or phrase in all capitals in the Sherlock Holmes quotation below is contained within the group of letters. Words can be found horizontally, vertically, or diagonally. They may read either forward or backward.

It is CONJECTURED that he may have been HURRYING DOWN to catch the LAST TRAIN from WATERLOO STATION, and that in his HASTE and the EXTREME DARKNESS he missed his PATH and walked over the EDGE of one of the small LANDING-PLACES for river STEAMBOATS. The body EXHIBITED no TRACES OF VIOLENCE, and there can be no doubt that the DECEASED had been the victim of an UNFORTUNATE ACCIDENT, which should have the effect of calling the ATTENTION of the AUTHORITIES to the CONDITION of the RIVERSIDE landing-STAGES.' "

```
X E S D U M A S G D O N N E R X Z E X
N G E X T R E M E D A R K N E S S C F
W W G R F X I S Q Y O N M A A F K Y Z
O L A A O A A P B Z C Q J P W V V X E
D A T Q S E I T I R O H T U A O Y L G
G N S E C D U V M E X H I B I T E D D
N D C E I A A Y G W F C N D Q T H Q E
I I D O N O I T A T S O O L R E T A W
Y N S W N W T O R L S U I I H M M E Z
R G X T O J N Q A Q L G T B K J R D N
R P D W E J E S L J U Q I R L O V I O
U L F F Y A T C V O Z N D H M E C S I
H A S T E T M U T S X F N M E T L R T
P C N B R Z H B R U F D O E T D F E N
J E P A N J F V O U R A C E B A A V E
V S I U S C O X Q A J E S F A Z A I T
U N T I W W L T M W T K D W A C V R T
Q E C N E L O I V F O S E C A R T O A
U N F O R T U N A T E A C C I D E N T
```

Answers on page 382.

The Five Orange Pips Passage 1

Each word or phrase in all capitals in the Sherlock Holmes quotation below is contained within the group of letters. Words can be found horizontally, vertically, or diagonally. They may read either forward or backward.

It was in the LATTER DAYS of SEPTEMBER, and the EQUINOCTIAL GALES had set in with EXCEPTIONAL violence. ALL DAY the WIND had SCREAMED and the rain had BEATEN against the WINDOWS, so that even here in the HEART of great, HAND-MADE London we were FORCED to raise our minds for the INSTANT from the ROUTINE OF LIFE and to RECOGNISE the PRESENCE of those great ELEMENTAL FORCES which SHRIEK at MANKIND through the bars of his CIVILISATION, like UNTAMED BEASTS in a CAGE.

```
N Q G H C M B R V Z N E T A E B N L K
U N T A M E D B E A S T S L C J Q J R
P E Q O K H B V F P Z G E B A A L T X
Q L D C X U G O L M A M C V G N B S T
E A S A V B R O V A E Y D H E W S U E
K N C U M C A C X N M E T B R Y U S F
E O S S E D Q W T V M Y B Q A B A T I
W I T D K W N A E A R Y J D K S A E L
I T R A U L L A E D J K R J O Z S S F
N P A N L F H R H P R E S E N C E I O
D E E J O L C C L Y T S M I J T D N E
O C H R C S D L C T H S R R A V N G N
W X C W R K B A A T N A T S N I I O I
S E V K V E H L Y E F R L G K B K C T
S R A I S E D O U R M I N D S A N E U
N N O I T A S I L I V I C L K E A R O
E Q U I N O C T I A L G A L E S M H R
Z R R D N I W S H R I E K C G S S P N
S E P T E M B E R O T Z O L P U E T J
```

Answers on page 382.

The Five Orange Pips Passage 2

Each word or phrase in all capitals in the Sherlock Holmes quotation below is contained within the group of letters. Words can be found horizontally, vertically, or diagonally. They may read either forward or backward.

There is EVER A FLAW, however, in the BEST LAID of HUMAN PLANS, and the MURDERERS of John Openshaw were NEVER to receive the ORANGE PIPS which would show them that another, as CUNNING and as RESOLUTE as themselves, was UPON THEIR TRACK. Very long and VERY SEVERE were the equinoctial gales THAT YEAR. We WAITED LONG for news of the Lone Star of SAVAN-NAH, but none ever reached us. We did at LAST HEAR that some-where far out in the ATLANTIC a shattered STERN-POST of a boat was seen SWINGING in the TROUGH OF A WAVE, with the letters "L. S." CARVED upon it, and that is all which we shall ever know of the FATE of the Lone Star.

```
H U M A N P L A N S V H H U G E Z
Z Z T S O P N R E T S W D I N X D
F K O L Z F Q R V Z T V F Y I T E
P M C E I V M D A Q Z E Q X G P O
K W U A G N O L D E T I A W N T H
V A Q V R N P R J U H A X U I B A
E L E J E T K C L H P T N O W L G
R F A V K J R O G B I D S R S N H
Y A E Y W Z S I H V B B Z A I C A
S R B A Z E K F E E O Q S N L I N
E E C A R V E D S H Q U N G A T N
V V H B P Z A T F J T U D E G N A
E E E N A P L M A T C N T P V A V
R A E Y T A H T T A F E O I G L A
E B V E I U W G E Y C B X P E T S
M U R D E R E R S Y J E N S U A D
T R O U G H O F A W A V E N J Y K
```

333   *Answers on page 383.*

Famous First Lines

How well do you know the Holmes canon? Match the first line of each story to the story's title.

1. On glancing over my notes of the seventy odd cases in which I have during the last eight years studied the methods of my friend Sherlock Holmes, I find many tragic, some comic, a large number merely strange, but none commonplace; for, working as he did rather for the love of his art than for the acquirement of wealth, he refused to associate himself with any investigation which did not tend towards the unusual, and even the fantastic.

2. We were seated at breakfast one morning, my wife and I, when the maid brought in a telegram.

3. It is years since the incidents of which I speak took place, and yet it is with diffidence that I allude to them.

4. I had called upon my friend Sherlock Holmes upon the second morning after Christmas, with the intention of wishing him the compliments of the season.

5. An anomaly which often struck me in the character of my friend Sherlock Holmes was that, although in his methods of thought he was the neatest and most methodical of mankind, and although also he affected a certain quiet primness of dress, he was none the less in his personal habits one of the most untidy men that ever drove a fellow-lodger to distraction.

A. The Adventure of the Blue Carbuncle

B. The Adventure of the Musgrave Ritual

C. The Boscombe Valley Mystery

D. The Adventure of Charles Augustus Milverton

E. The Adventure of the Speckled Band

Answers on page 383.

Fill in the Empty House

Fill in the blank! Complete each quote from the Sherlock Holmes story "The Empty House" with one of the choices.

1. A minute examination of the circumstances served only to make the case more _____.

    A. bizarre   **B.** complex   **C.** obvious

2. With a snarl of contempt he turned upon his heel, and I saw his curved back and white _____ disappear among the throng.

    A. side-whiskers   **B.** beard   **C.** head

3. "Well, then, about that _____. I had no serious difficulty in getting out of it, for the very simple reason that I never was in it."

    A. chasm   **B.** bog   **C.** abyss

4. "_____ is the best antidote to sorrow, my dear Watson," said he; "and I have a piece of work for us both to-night which, if we can bring it to a successful conclusion, will in itself justify a man's life on this planet."

    A. labor   **B.** success   **C.** work

5. Am I such a(n) _____, Watson, that I should erect an obvious dummy, and expect that some of the sharpest men in Europe would be deceived by it?"

    A. silly fool   **B.** farcical bungler   **C.** obvious idiot

Answers on page 383.

The Adventure of the Golden Pince-Nez

Each word or phrase in all capitals in the Sherlock Holmes quotation below is contained within the group of letters. Words can be found horizontally, vertically, or diagonally. They may read either forward or backward.

It was a wild, TEMPESTUOUS night, towards the close of NOVEMBER. Holmes and I sat together in silence all the EVENING, he engaged with a powerful lens DECIPHERING the remains of the original INSCRIPTION upon a PALIMPSEST, I deep in a recent TREATISE upon SURGERY. Outside the wind HOWLED down Baker Street, while the rain beat FIERCELY against the windows. It was strange there, in the very depths of the town, with ten miles of man's HANDIWORK on every side of us, to feel the iron grip of NATURE, and to be conscious that to the huge ELEMENTAL forces all London was no more than the molehills that dot the fields. I walked to the window, and looked out on the DESERTED street. The occasional lamps gleamed on the expanse of MUDDY road and shining pavement. A single CAB was SPLASHING its way from the OXFORD STREET end.

```
U T E M P E S T U O U S J G E
G G M Q B T J N T H X E U N S
G N I R E H P I C E D D L I I
P I G D E S E R T E D A O N T
A H Q Z B H L S D E T X N E A
L S U K G P U E R N F O R V E
I A X G V R L U E O I E C E R
M L Q F G W T M R T B B Q O T
P P Z E O A E D P M X P A Z U
S S R H N L S I E L B R E C D
E Y S W E T R V G K E P M R E
S Z B R R C O F I E R C E L Y
T U R E S N W B W I M U D D Y
X A E N S S K R O W I D N A H
C T I X S V Q M H B S P S D F
```

 Answers on page 383.

International Fugitives

This was a busy week for Interpol, the international law enforcement agency. Five different criminals from the international "10 Most Wanted" list were apprehended, each in a different country and on a different day. None of the five committed the same crime. Using only the clues below, match each captured fugitive to his crime, and determine the date and location (country) in which he was finally apprehended.

1. Cal Calumnet wasn't apprehended in France.

2. The robbery suspect was captured 3 days before Ben Blackforth.

3. Gil Grendle was wanted for either robbery or arson.

4. Of Ben Blackforth and whoever was captured on October 7th, one was wanted for the arson and the other was tracked down in Sweden.

5. The October 5th capture was of either Cal Calumnet or the man wanted for tax evasion.

6. The forger was captured 2 days before the arrest in Uganda.

7. The arrest in France occurred sometime after that of Dale Dornmer.

8. Neither Dale Dornmer nor Cal Calumnet was captured in Peru.

	Criminals					Crimes					Countries				
	Blackforth	Calumnet	Dornmer	Filcher	Grendle	Arson	Blackmail	Forgery	Robbery	Tax evasion	France	Moldova	Peru	Sweden	Uganda
Dates October 3															
October 4															
October 5															
October 6															
October 7															
Countries France															
Moldova															
Peru															
Sweden															
Uganda															
Crimes Arson															
Blackmail															
Forgery															
Robbery															
Tax evasion															

Dates	Criminals	Crimes	Countries
October 3			
October 4			
October 5			
October 6			
October 7			

Answers on page 383.

Charles Augustus Milverton

Each word or phrase in all capitals in the Sherlock Holmes quotation below is contained within the group of letters. Words can be found horizontally, vertically, or diagonally. They may read either forward or backward.

"Hum! He's about due. Do you feel a CREEPING, shrinking sensation, Watson, when you stand before the SERPENTS in the Zoo, and see the SLITHERY, GLIDING, VENOMOUS creatures, with their DEADLY eyes and WICKED, flattened faces? Well, that's how MILVERTON impresses me. I've had to do with fifty MURDERERS in my career, but the worst of them never gave me the REPULSION which I have for this fellow. And yet I can't get out of doing BUSINESS with him—indeed, he is here at my INVITATION."

"But who is he?"

"I'll tell you, Watson. He is the KING of all the BLACKMAILERS. Heaven help the man, and still more the woman, whose SECRET and REPUTATION come into the POWER of Milverton! With a SMILING face and a HEART of MARBLE, he will SQUEEZE and squeeze until he has DRAINED them dry."

```
H N D V J B S U O M O N E V M Y T
C S M I L I N G Q N S K Q R A E U
T R S G H J G Y E A R O M O R F E
R U E D L S S Q U E E Z E C B K N
A R R E L I F Z G Z L W E P L S K
E Q P C P M D E T Z I S Z D E R F
H Y E B S I E I K P A W I C K E D
Q S N U A P N F N W M N N F R R R
E L T K V G I G D G K O V P E E E
S I S U N B A X Y J C I I B W D P
R T L H P B R G E K A S T U O R U
K H P E E M D G I G L L A S P U T
I E J O L E F B G L B U T I R M A
N R D H A B A H P M W P I N A B T
G Y K D L D X O V Q U E O E W T I
M I L V E R T O N R S R N S B I O
W Y Q B T I E H H U U F P S C L N
```

Answers on page 383.

Solve a Crime

Change just one letter on each line to go from the top word to the bottom word. Do not change the order of the letters. You must have a common English word at each step.

CRIME

_____

_____

_____

_____

_____ Opposite of losses, sometimes ill-gotten

_____

_____

_____

_____

_____ To harass or attack, also a male name

_____

_____

_____

_____

_____

_____

_____

SOLVE

Murder Mysteries

Change just one letter on each line to go from the top word to the bottom word. Do not change the order of the letters. You must have a common English word at each step.

MURDERS

_____ players or racehorses that do well on a wet, muddy field

_____ a perennial herb (plural form)

_____

_____

_____

_____

_____

_____

_____

_____ those who read

_____

_____

_____

_____

_____ baseball players

_____

_____

_____

MYSTERY

 Answers on page 383.

The Murderous Gem Thief

5 types of gems were stolen from the murder scene. There was 1 gem of the first type, 2 of the second type, 3 of the third type, 4 of the fourth type, and 5 of the fifth type. From the information given below, can you tell how many gemstones of each kind were taken?

1. There are twice as many pearls as diamonds, but fewer pearls than pieces of jade.

2. Rubies are not the rarest gem.

3. There are an even number of sapphires.

4. Rubies are not the most plentiful gem.

Murder Method: Shot by Guns

Change just one letter on each line to go from the top word to the bottom word. Do not change the order of the letters. You must have a common English word at each step.

SHOT

_____

_____

_____

_____

_____

_____

_____

_____

GUNS

Answers on page 384.

Answers

A "Smell Oh Shocker" Anagram
(page 4)

I had neither kith nor kin in England, and was therefore as free as Air—or as free as an INCOME of eleven shillings and sixpence a day will PERMIT a man to be. Under such circumstances, I naturally gravitated to London, that great CESSPOOL into which all the LOUNGERS and idlers of the Empire are irresistibly drained. There I stayed for some time at a PRIVATE hotel in the Strand, leading a COMFORT-LESS, meaningless existence, and spending such money as I had, considerably more FREELY than I ought. So ALARMING did the state of my FINANCES become, that I soon realized that I must either leave the metropolis and RUSTICATE somewhere in the country, or that I must make a complete ALTERATION in my style of living. Choosing the latter alternative, I began by making up my mind to leave the hotel, and to take up my quarters in some less PRETENTIOUS and less expensive DOMICILE.

BONUS ANSWER: "A Study in Scarlet"

What Do You See? (pages 5–6)
Picture 1 is a match.

A "Sol Ohm Hecklers" Anagram
(page 7)

"Really, Watson, you excel YOUR-SELF," said Holmes, pushing back his chair and lighting a cigarette. "I am bound to say that in all the AC-COUNTS which you have been so good as to give of my own small ACHIEVEMENTS you have habitually UNDERRATED your own abilities. It may be that you are not yourself LUMINOUS, but you are a conductor of light. Some people without POS-SESSING genius have a remarkable power of STIMULATING it. I confess, my dear FELLOW, that I am very much in your debt."

BONUS ANSWER: "The Hound of the Baskervilles"

Famous First Lines (page 8)
1. C; 2. D; 3. A; 4. B. 5. E

What Changed? (pages 9–10)
The hammer changed positions.

What Went Missing? (pages 11–12)
The frame above the mantelpiece disappeared (the documents were taped to the back of it).

Tracking the Hound of the Baskervilles (page 13)

1. B; 2. A 3. B; 4. C; 5. B

The Hound of the Baskervilles (pages 14–15)

A Sad Statistic (page 16)

The percentage of stolen art that is recovered is not very high. Only five to ten percent might be recovered.

What Went Missing? (pages 17–18)

All the books on the top right shelf have gone missing. The documents were hidden in one of them.

What Went Missing? (pages 19–20)

The hand spade went missing.

A Study in Sherlock (page 21)

1. A; 2. C; 3. B; 4. A; 5. C

The Hound of the Baskervilles Characters (pages 22–23)

The Curse of the Baskervilles Pt. 1 (pages 24–25)

The Curse of the Baskervilles
Pt. 2 (pages 26–27)

The Curse of the Baskervilles
Pt. 4 (pages 30–31)

The Curse of the Baskervilles
Pt. 3 (pages 28–29)

The Curse of the Baskervilles
Pt. 5 (pages 32–33)

The Curse of the Baskervilles
Pt. 6 (pages 34–35)

The Curse of the Baskervilles
Pt. 8 (pages 38–39)

The Curse of the Baskervilles
Pt. 7 (pages 36–37)

The Curse of the Baskervilles
Pt. 9 (pages 40–41)

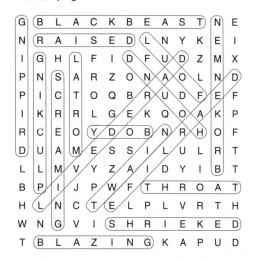

The Curse of the Baskervilles Pt. 10 (pages 42–43)

A "Her Loss Hemlock" Anagram
(page 44)

"It is SIMPLICITY itself," he remarked, chuckling at my surprise,–"so ABSURDLY simple that an explanation is SUPERFLUOUS; and yet it may serve to define the limits of OBSERVATION and of DEDUCTTION. OBSERVATION tells me that you have a little reddish mould ADHERING to your instep. Just OPPOSITE the Seymour Street Office they have taken up the PAVEMENT and thrown up some earth which lies in such a way that it is difficult to avoid TREADING in it in entering. The earth is of this peculiar REDDISH tint which is found, as far as I know, NOWHERE else in the neighborhood. So much is OBSERVATION. The rest is DEDUCTION."

"How, then, did you deduce the TELEGRAM _____?"

"Why, of course I knew that you had not WRITTEN a letter, since I sat opposite to you all MORNING. I see also in your open desk there that you have a sheet of stamps and a thick bundle of post-cards. What could you go into the post-office for, then, but to send a wire? ELIMINATE all other FACTORS, and the one which REMAINS must be the truth."

BONUS ANSWER: "The Sign of the Four"

What Went Missing? (pages 45–46)

The bottles and jars on the 4th shelf down on the right had all been taken.

A "Ms Holler Chokes" Anagram
(page 47)

"Porlock, Watson, is a NOM-DE-PLUME, a mere identification mark; but behind it lies a shifty and EVASIVE personality. In a former letter he FRANKLY informed me that the name was not his own, and DEFIED me ever to trace him among the TEEMING millions of this great city. Porlock is important, not for HIMSELF, but for the great man with whom he is in touch. PICTURE to yourself the pilot fish with the SHARK, the jackal with the lion—anything that is insignificant in companionship with what is FOR-

MIDABLE: not only FORMIDABLE, Watson, but SINISTER—in the highest degree SINISTER. That is where he comes within my purview. You have heard me speak of PROFESSOR MORIARTY?"

BONUS ANSWER: "The Valley of Fear"

Interception (page 48)

Take the central letter of each word and you get ALINAM. Flip this, and it becomes MANILA

Crack the Password (page 49)

The missing letter is S.

monster, passion, relapse, scullery

For Stage and Screen
(pages 50–51)

D	O	N	A	L	D	P	I	C	K	E	R	I	N	G
A	K	K	B	N	B	R	U	C	E	M	C	R	A	E
V	R	A	Y	M	O	N	D	F	R	A	N	C	I	S
I	Q	Y	X	O	C	N	A	L	A	Q	Q	Y	R	R
D	G	N	U	O	Y	D	N	A	L	O	R	W	O	F
B	E	N	K	I	N	G	S	L	E	Y	H	F	B	B
U	I	N	I	G	E	L	B	R	U	C	E	X	E	V
R	T	R	H	T	F	Q	S	C	D	Q	J	S	R	M
K	W	P	O	J	X	D	Y	R	Y	U	V	I	T	H
E	K	C	I	W	D	R	A	H	D	R	A	W	D	E
M	A	R	T	I	N	F	R	E	E	M	A	N	U	I
W	E	L	L	E	B	E	L	R	Y	K	H	C	V	T
H	X	E	E	N	C	A	M	K	C	I	R	T	A	P
S	I	L	L	I	W	T	R	E	B	U	H	M	L	V
W	J	M	C	O	L	I	N	B	L	A	K	E	L	Y

Interception (page 52)

Take the central letter of each word and you reveal LONDON.

A "Shh Mole Locker" Anagram
(page 53)

"You will remember that I remarked the other day, just before we went into the very SIMPLE problem presented by Miss Mary Sutherland, that for strange effects and EXTRAORDINARY combinations we must go to life itself, which is always far more DARING than any effort of the IMAGINATION."

"A proposition which I took the LIBERTY of DOUBTING."

"You did, DOCTOR, but none the less you must come round to my view, for otherwise I shall keep on PILING fact upon fact on you until your reason breaks down under them and ACKNOWLEDGES me to be right. Now, Mr. Jabez Wilson here has been good enough to call upon me this morning, and to begin a NARRATIVE which promises to be one of the most SINGULAR which I have listened to for some time. You have heard me remark that the STRANGEST and most unique things are very often CONNECTED not with the larger but with the smaller CRIMES, and occasionally, indeed, where there is room for doubt whether any POSITIVE crime has been committed. As far as I have heard it is IMPOSSIBLE for

me to say whether the present case is an INSTANCE of crime or not, but the course of events is CERTAINLY among the most SINGULAR that I have ever listened to."

BONUS ANSWER: "The Red-Headed League"

A Study in Sherlock (page 54)

1. Nil; 2. Nil; 3. Nil; 4. Feeble; 5. Variable (Watson further describes his botanical knowledge as "Well up in belladonna, opium, and poisons generally. Knows nothing of practical gardening."); 6. Practical, but limited. 7. Profound; 8. Accurate, but unsystematic; 9. Immense.

Crack the Password (page 55)

The missing letter is P.

clapper, desperate, flipper, input

Famous First Lines (page 56)

1. B; 2. D; 3. E; 4. A; 5. C

A "Chrome Elk Slosh" Anagram (page 57)

To Sherlock Holmes she is always THE woman. I have seldom heard him MENTION her under any other name. In his eyes she ECLIPSES and predominates the whole of her sex. It was not that he felt any EMOTION akin to love for Irene Adler. All EMOTIONS, and that one particularly, were ABHORRENT to his cold, precise but admirably BALANCED mind. He was, I take it, the most perfect reasoning and observing MACHINE that the world has seen, but as a lover he would have placed himself in a false POSITION. He never spoke of the softer PASSIONS, save with a gibe and a sneer. They were ADMIRABLE things for the observer—excellent for drawing the veil from men's MOTIVES and actions. But for the trained reasoner to admit such INTRUSTIONS into his own delicate and finely adjusted TEMPERAMENT was to introduce a distracting factor which might throw a doubt upon all his mental results. Grit in a sensitive INSTRUMENT, or a crack in one of his own high-power lenses, would not be more DISTURBING than a strong emotion in a nature such as his. And yet there was but one woman to him, and that woman was the late Irene Adler, of dubious and QUESTIONABLE memory.

BONUS ANSWER: "A Scandal in Bohemia"

A Mysterious Event (page 58)

The year 1911 involved a notable case of art theft—the Mona Lisa was stolen from the Louvre by an employee. He was caught two years later and the painting was returned to its home.

Interception (page 59)

Take the last letter of each place name to reveal: CHICAGO

A "Clerks Shoo Helm" Anagram (page 60)

"My dear fellow," said Sherlock Holmes as we sat on either side of the fire in his LODGINGS at Baker Street, "life is INFINITELY stranger than anything which the mind of man could INVENT. We would not dare to CONCEIVE the things which are really mere COMMONPLACES of existence. If we could fly out of that WINDOW hand in hand, hover over this great city, gently REMOVE the roofs, and peep in at the queer things which are going on, the strange COINCIDENCES, the plannings, the cross-purposes, the WONDERFUL chains of events, working through GENERATIONS, and leading to the most outré results, it would make all fiction with its conventionalities and FORESEEN conclusions most stale and UNPROFITABLE."

BONUS ANSWER: "A Case of Identity"

Interception (page 61)

Take the central letter of each word in the phrase and you get: ESUOHE-FAS, CED, TSRIF, MPENO. Read each item backwards and you get: safehouse, Dec. first, One PM.

Nothing to Do with Doyle (page 62)

H.H. Holmes wasn't a fictional detective—he was a serial killer, often considered the first in America. Born Herman Webster Mudgett in 1861, he confessed to 27 murders but may have been responsible for more. He was also a bigamist, married to three women at the time of his death.

A "Oh Shell Mockers" Anagram (page 63)

"CIRCUMSTANTIAL EVIDENCE is a very tricky thing," answered Holmes thoughtfully. "It may seem to point very STRAIGHT to one thing, but if you shift your own point of view a little, you may find it pointing in an equally UNCOMPROMISING manner to something entirely different. It must be confessed, however, that the case looks EXCEEDINGLY grave against the young man, and it is very possible that he is indeed the CULPRIT. There are several people in the neighbourhood, however, and among them Miss Turner, the daughter of the neighbouring LANDOWNER, who believe in his INNOCENCE, and who have RETAINED Lestrade, whom you may recollect in connection with the Study in SCARLET, to work out the case in his interest. Lestrade, being rather puzzled, has REFERRED the case to me, and hence it is that two middle-aged GENTLEMEN are flying WESTWARD at fifty miles an hour

instead of quietly DIGESTING their BREAKFASTS at home."

BONUS ANSWER: "The Boscombe Valley Mystery"

The Women of Sherlock Holmes
(pages 64–65)

```
X A F R A C S E C N A R F  F I
M A R Y S U T H E R L A N D  F
Y A L C R A B Y C N A N  K Z K
S U S A N C U S H I N G  U C H
A K R E T N U H T E L O I V  T
A Y L E F F I E M U N R O  I I
B H M A R Y M O R S T A N  R M
V H A T T Y D O R A N  F R E S
B E R Y L S T A P L E T O N  T
V B L U C Y F E R R I E R  E E
A C C U L A I L I M E  U C A L
H E L E N S T O N E R  E N D O
E V A B L A C K W E L L  T L I
S O T E C K O D E P E T Q E  V
X E L I Z A B A R R Y M O R E
```

Famous Last Lines (page 66)
1. E; 2. B; 3. C; 4. D. 5. A

Famous Last Lines (page 67)
1. D; 2. C; 3. A; 4. B. 5. E

The Hound of the Baskervilles Passage 1 (pages 68–69)

```
I C C C O N D U C T O R E S H
S U O N I M U L B U Y R Y T K
Z M N G W L Q E T D U N J N D
J R F B X P D K R D Y S V E E
I D E A C C O U N T S Y E M T
M Q S J V B F C H L Q R E E T
K I S W S B O O K L F T Y Y E
R E W O P E L B A K R A M E R
S W Y V Q E I U C M T G U I A
E Q G L V Q T T T F L G C H G
M J G I L I T M I C P E H C I
L M F W B A J X H L V Z C A C
O D D A H V E A G I I M K X O
H D H T N R I R U U B B S Q E
Q H D D W R R Z E F L G A L G
```

The Hound of the Baskervilles Passage 2 (pages 70–71)

```
R Y I Y B R Z H T I N G E L V
I L G J S T F I R D F X A H Y
E O G N W P G V G A G N B E E
H H V F I L H F U Y E H Q V L
G C C O U N T R Y S I D E O L
N N I U W S A E R U T A N R O
I A Q Q O P T W K B G T V D W
N L F L U T T E R E D C R V L
R E A Y V E G E T A T I O N E
U M S L E E H W S U I X I U A
T R I D C C Z H S T R D H T V
E S I Y N G S K T I V Q Q N E
R A T T L E C X F F Q P C H S
C A R R I A G E I U W S G H X
G L O C W P L S G L G E Y E S
```

354

The Hound of the Baskervilles Passage 3 (pages 72–73)

The Hound of the Baskervilles Passage 4 (pages 74–75)

A "Shh Cooker Smell" Anagram (page 76)

It was difficult to REFUSE any of Sherlock Holmes' requests, for they were always so exceedingly DEFINITE, and put forward with such a quiet air of MASTERY. I felt, however, that when Whitney was once CONFINED in the cab my mission was practically ACCOMPLISHED; and for the rest, I could not wish anything better than to be ASSOCIATED with my friend in one of those singular ADVENTURES which were the normal condition of his EXISTENCE. In a few minutes I had written my note, paid Whitney's bill, led him out to the cab, and seen him driven through the DARKNESS. In a very short time a DECREPIT figure had emerged from the OPIUM DEN, and I was walking down the street with Sherlock Holmes. For two streets he SHUFFLED along with a bent back and an UNCERTAIN foot. Then, glancing quickly round, he straightened himself out and burst into a HEARTY fit of laughter.

BONUS ANSWER: "The Man with the Twisted Lip"

What Went Missing? (pages 77–78)

The compass went missing.

A "Shh Cello Smoker" Anagram (page 79)

"No, no. No crime," said Sherlock Holmes, laughing. "Only one of those WHIMSICAL little INCIDENTS which will happen when you have four million human beings all JOSTLING each other within the space of a few square miles. Amid the action and reaction of so dense a swarm of HUMANITY, every possible COMBINATION of events may be expected to take place, and many a little problem will be presented which may be STRIKING and BIZARRE without being criminal. We have ALREADY had experience of such."

BONUS ANSWER: "The Adventure of the Blue Carbuncle"

Art Thefts (pagse 80–81)

Months	Titles	Artists	Museums
April	City Dreams	De Lorenzo	Givernelle
May	Apple Cart	Strauss	Tendrille
June	Elba at Dawn	Pocalini	Beaufort
July	Madame V.	Lafayette	Millefoi

The Empty House (pages 82–83)

```
S R B J C J H A Q U I L I N E
N P D J H C B L K D Q G H P R
L Z T T T G D Q I M T I O M M
H E K E T O K H J Q H I S E P
A H R E S J B F Y N M A N K Y
V T H T I R I P S H K K G B
S X N T N K M L A C L W I O E
H X O T E M D F L E A C L K L
V W I E W L I U M F T L R K I
S P N J Y D F J P W W U I C E
H E E B M D P R Y D E E S V V
R E T N A H C R E M K O O B E
T K U E T H I N N E R H S L Q
F V R H M F A R N P V A W X U
H D A J U S A H S T A T U R E
```

Interception (page 84)

Take the second letter of each word and you reveal: BUCHAREST

What Changed? (Part II) (page 86)

The meat fork was flipped.

A Seeker of Truth (page 87)

In the 1930s, Bengali writer Sharadindu Bandyopadhyay introduced a character named Byomkesh Bakshi, who solved mysteries but preferred the term "truth-seeker" to detective. The character appeared in 32 stories in the decades that followed, and inspired a television show and several movies. He's been called "The Indian Sherlock Holmes."

Passing Bad Checks (pages 88–89)

Dates	Stores	Towns	Amounts
October 2	Carpet City	Rio Pondo	$125.12
October 6	Well Mart	Georgetown	$85.50
October 10	Quick-Stop	Appleton	$52.89
October 14	David's Deli	Lincoln	$35.15

The Final Problem (pages 90–91)

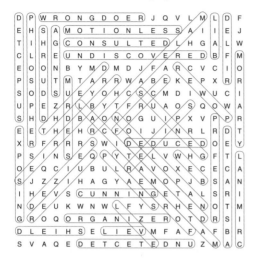

A "Hock Meshes Roll" Anagram
(page 92)

"It is not cold which makes me shiver," said the woman in a low voice, changing her seat as REQUESTED.

"What, then?"

"It is fear, Mr. Holmes. It is TERROR." She raised her veil as she spoke, and we could see that she was indeed in a PITIABLE state of AGITATION, her face all drawn and grey, with restless FRIGHTENED eyes, like those of some hunted animal. Her FEATURES and figure were those of a woman of thirty, but her hair was shot with PRE-MATURE grey, and her expression was weary and HAGGARD. Sherlock Holmes ran her over with one of his quick, all-comprehensive glances.

"You must not fear," said he SOOTH-INGLY, bending forward and patting her FOREARM. "We shall soon set matters right, I have no DOUBT. You have come in by TRAIN this morning, I see."

BONUS ANSWER: "The Adventure of the Speckled Band"

What Do You See? (pages 93–94)
Picture 2 is a match.

A "Lock Helm Horses" Anagram
(page 95)

He was a man of about fifty, tall, PORTLY, and imposing, with a massive, strongly marked face and a COMMANDING figure. He was dressed in a sombre yet rich style, in black FROCK-COAT, shining hat, neat brown GAITERS, and well-cut pearl-grey TROUSERS. Yet his actions were in absurd contrast to the DIG-NITY of his dress and features, for he was running hard, with OCCASION-AL little springs, such as a weary man gives who is little ACCUSTOMED to set any tax upon his legs. As he ran he jerked his hands up and down, waggled his head, and WRITHED his face into the most extraordinary CONTOR-TIONS.

BONUS ANSWER: "The Adventure of the Beryl Coronet"

The Missing Millionaire (pages 96–97)

Days	Witnesses	Cities	States
Tuesday	Edna Eddel	Ballingford	Nevada
Wednesday	Hilda Hayes	Tetley	California
Thursday	Susie Seuss	Ventura	Washington
Friday	Walt Wolsen	Pescadero	Oregon

The Adventure of the Blue Carbuncle (pages 98–99)

The Adventure of the Blue Carbuncle Passage 1 (pages 100–101)

The Adventure of the Blue Carbuncle Description Pt. 1 (pages 102–103)

The Adventure of the Blue Carbuncle Description Pt. 2 (pages 104–105)

The Adventure of the Blue Carbuncle Newspaper Ad Pt. 1
(pages 106–107)

The Adventure of the Blue Carbuncle Newspaper Ad Pt. 2
(pages 108–109)

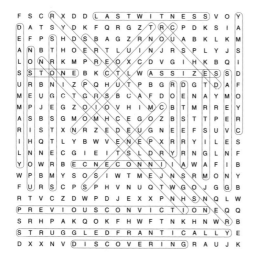

Thinking Things Through (page 110)

"There are two questions waiting for us at the outset. The one is whether any crime has been committed at all; the second is, what is the crime and how was it committed? Of course, if Dr. Mortimer's surmise should be correct, and we are dealing with forces outside the ordinary laws of Nature, there is an end of our investigation. But we are bound to exhaust all other hypotheses before falling back upon this one. I think we'll shut that window again, if you don't mind. It is a singular thing, but I find that a concentrated atmosphere helps a concentration of thought. I have not pushed it to the length of getting into a box to think, but that is the logical outcome of my convictions."

BONUS ANSWER: Sherlock Holmes in "The Hound of the Baskervilles"

What Do You See? (pages 111–112)

1. Two, numbered 1 and 4; 2. Wineglass; 3. Fork; 4. True; 5. True

Fingerprint Match (page 113)

The matching pairs are: A and S; B and V; C and P; D and M; E and O; F and G; H and T; I and R; J and X; K and W; L and U; N and Q

Anna's Alibis (pages 114–115)

Times	Alibis	Relations	Locations
8:00pm	Penny Pugh	neighbor	Delancey Rd.
8:30pm	Lina Lopez	friend	First St.
9:00pm	Norma Neet	co-worker	Ewing Ave.
9:30pm	Maddy Meyer	bartender	Capitol St.
10:00pm	Oda Osborn	cousin	Border Ln.

The "Gloria Scott" (pages 116–117)

A "Mocks Shell Hero" Anagram
(page 118)

"Pshaw, my dear fellow, what do the public, the great UNOBSERVANT public, who could hardly tell a WEAVER by his tooth or a compositor by his left thumb, care about the finer shades of ANALYSIS and deduction! But, indeed, if you are TRIVIAL, I cannot blame you, for the days of the great cases are past. Man, or at least criminal man, has lost all ENTERPRISE and ORIGINALITY. As to my own little practice, it seems to be

DEGENERATING into an agency for recovering lost lead pencils and giving ADVICE to young ladies from boarding-schools. I think that I have touched bottom at last, however. This note I had this morning marks my zero-point, I fancy. Read it!" He tossed a CRUMPLED letter across to me.

BONUS ANSWER: "The Adventure of the Copper Beeches"

A "Hello Her Smocks" Anagram
(page 119)

"It is one of those cases where the art of the REASONER should be used rather for the SIFTING of DETAILS than for the acquiring of fresh EVIDENCE. The tragedy has been so uncommon, so complete and of such PERSONAL importance to so many people, that we are suffering from a PLETHORA of surmise, conjecture, and HYPOTHESIS. The difficulty is to DETACH the framework of fact—of absolute UNDENIABLE fact—from the embellishments of THEORISTS and reporters. Then, having established ourselves upon this sound basis, it is our duty to see what INFERENCES may be drawn and what are the SPECIAL points upon which the whole mystery turns."

BONUS ANSWER: "The Adventure of Silver Blaze"

The Escape Artist (pages 120–121)

Years	Prisons	States	Methods
2001	Middle Fork	Alabama	wire cutters
2005	Tulveride	Idaho	uniform
2009	Pennington	Montana	tunnel
2013	Lexington	Virginia	ladder
2017	Calahatchee	Colorado	rope

For Stage and Screen (pages 122-123)

The Adventures of Sherlock Holmes Stories (pages 124–125)

For His Generation (page 126)

One of the most famous portrayals of Holmes came from Basil Rathbone in the Forties. Rathbone played the detective in fourteen films. Earlier films were set in Victorian times, while some of the later installations were set in the Forties, with plots related to the second World War. There was also a radio series.

What Went Missing? (pages 127–128)

The lipstick went missing.

Rental Agreements (page 129)

Not only was her first-floor flat invaded at all hours by throngs of singular and often undesirable characters but her remarkable lodger showed an eccentricity and irregularity in his life which must have sorely tried her patience. His incredible untidiness, his addiction to music at strange hours, his occasional revolver practice within doors, his weird and often malodorous scientific experiments, and the atmosphere of violence and danger which hung around him made him the very worst tenant in London. On the other hand, his payments were princely.

BONUS ANSWER: Mrs. Hudson and Sherlock Holmes are described in "The Adventure of the Dying Detective"

Fingerprint Match (page 130)

H is the matching fingerprint.

Fingerprint Match (page 131)

Q and W are the matching fingerprints.

In Other Words (page 132)

Synonyms for mysterious include secret, enigmatic, furtive, shadowy, cryptic, and clandestine.

Interception (page 133)

Take the first letter and the last letter of each word to reveal: WASHINGTON DC

A "Cork Shell Homes" Anagram (page 134)

Sherlock Holmes was a man who seldom took EXERCISE for EXERCISE'S sake. Few men were capable of greater MUSCULAR effort, and he was UNDOUBTEDLY one of the finest boxers of his WEIGHT that I have ever seen; but he looked upon aimless bodily EXERTION as a waste of energy, and he seldom BESTIRRED himself save when there was some professional object to be served. Then he was absolutely UNTIRING and INDEFATIGABLE. That he should have kept himself in TRAINING under such CIRCUMSTANCES is remarkable, but his diet was usually of the SPAREST, and his habits were simple to the verge of AUSTERITY.

BONUS ANSWER: "The Adventure of the Yellow Face"

What Do You See? (pages 135–136)

Picture 3 is a match.

What Went Missing? (pages 137–138)

The brace went missing.

Everybody and His Brother (page 139)

Actor Christopher Lee played the famous detective in the 1962 movie *Sherlock Holmes and the Deadly Necklace*. In 1970, Lee played a Holmes again—Sherlock's brother Mycroft, in the movie *The Private Life of Sherlock Holmes*. He had also played Sir Henry Baskerville in an earlier film adapted from *The Hound of the Baskervilles*.

The Musgrave Ritual (pages 140–141)

```
D E B P Y A U A F O S N G T Z
X R I U R E T S U M W Y G B J
U N D O N A E A P F Z G P U J
R R I O H D O U T B U R S T S
C F S L C J L S R E P A P T E
B B E R O K I E G Y S H J E R
M W R M I I E S S G L T C R D
E L Z D X O V T E R A E H D N
R E L I C S M B K E C L N I M
R C U D O S U E W N I U N S U
E A I S C R V R M E M T Y H C
N S Y N N C H A M B E R S J O
W E Z E A X T N Q D H Q N E D
O S D H Z P G P Y O C A S T A
C D E T A L U M U C C A X H T
```

The Man with the Twisted Lip Letter (pages 146–147)

```
C G O M L N T S E R A E D I H
I R C W A T E R M A R K B I F
B A T D V Q M S Y A R J Y H H
E V A C W G V B I L S Q F U S
N E V I L L E P F L A P I G E
F S O A E J S D E I O M T E D
J E S C O C D R E N O J C E M
H N I T G P N S N M C A E R F
M D Z R O D A E E M M I R A E
E F E S B H B U I Q A U L O L
C B T A G G S Z F T D V G R L
D E K K W Y U W R S A O C R Y
D I R T Y T H U M B M P R Z L
O C C A B O T G N I W E H C E
F R I G H T E N E D O I Z T G
```

The Suspect List (pages 142–143)

Ages	Suspects	Professions	Towns
23	Vincent	lawyer	Midvale
26	Michael	engineer	Flagstaff
29	Nicholas	tennis pro	Billings
32	Albert	architect	Tulverton
35	Dennis	dentist	San Pedro

The Man with the Twisted Lip (pages 144–145)

```
Q Y Z L U B S M Y K O M W Y R
W G B G W E I A S W W Y Q B I
X R H E M G I O O A E O T R A
S A V K B G E D W N I Z T A L
L J J G W A K A T E F L E D C
W H D S E R J I S Q F A E S T
B U M E L J H W G V F I R T S
A G K X A W M T Y A X V T R E
R H E N A L M A D N A W S E L
O B D S O M S S J D P V R E L
F O I K T P A Y T M L S E T I
G O Q L Q T I V V B W Y K D V
O N M W V X V U Q C N F A T E
L E O F K Y T T M M S H B J N
D I R T Y S C O U N D R E L D
```

The Man with the Twisted Lip Passage 1 (pages 148–149)

```
R E P U L S I V E S N E E R E
F L E S M I H W E R H T I B E
I T F U G S A D F A C E D N R
O N I F T N I T N W O R B G T
C E L T O X Q Y U R O Q T H A
M M Y N I D E L G N A T G B M
P R M S E J E A U T E I Y A O
I E N U X E S L W S S L E B R
L L R D I Y D G I E A E R R F
L I E N D I Z T N H E C F U A K
O E U C V C O S P E S C R A
W V W H Q U B Z P B K O K R A
H E E L A S Y I F R S Q P M B
L B N Y M F S S Z H K C X Z S
N S M O O T H S K I N N E D J
```

The Man with the Twisted Lip
Passage 2 (pages 150–151)

```
U G W W E G S W A W C T H R O W N P E
N N L S T R A N G E H T S Q I X P E H
L O R I C M L M T A I L I N G O F F U
N S Y L M O N O T O N O U S N L C S U
O I Y X E R T S U L K C A L T L E C E X
I A G D N E W C O M E R U E E M H K W D
T G D F Z H O S M E G J S I M D A B L
A N C I C W J M H S X I P L U A O R U
S I D F Z H O S M E G J S I M D A B L
R D N E I G O B B Q H V E E S A W O E W A
E R R A L K L T B K P I P H P W X N A N
N U E G D O W O A I F T S U L M C T N E
N B T N I W U I P J T K Z S P Q G K E
O F T A M R D L J M C O W Z R X U N D
C U L U Z L F A N T A S T I C P O S E S
B G D N M L Y D E B J G R S
D N M L Y L I T T L E H E E D
C F C G E J X B R E D C I R C L E S T
U C L M E E B B W D U O T Z H S H O
```

The Man with the Twisted Lip
Confession Pt. 2 (pages 154–155)

```
P I L S L L A M S P I T I A B L E
S R I A H F O D A E H D E R G O N
R U G R E E N R O O M Y B W H Y X
U O T S I W T A N I P I L T Z Y L
O Z A T T A I N M E N T S F L B
H N O G T B S N F R T O O M L A I
N A E D O Q U I O A E F L E N M S
E D F A E D A I O T H U K J U E S
V A G D N C S U N C A I R R S T O
E S A O L T D R C O E N T Q N A S P
Y N V O E S N L A G S M S J E O I
F T R Y E D O V U R R S V C L D Z
H A W C N U A P P R O P R I A T E
V G C G R N Y T W T W E P E V K V
G E R E L L E S H C T A M D W R D
A A D W O T O M Y S U R P R I S E
```

The Man with the Twisted Lip
Confession Pt. 1 (pages 152–153)

```
G R E C I B P Y Q S E I W D J E S S J
B P T J O D E O L Y Q K Y F G E U P
B R U E T A M A X P D R F R I A L M B
L E D W I X M N S H P A B E D T C E X
B Y G E J A D V E N T U R E S S I T X
C W R G L N Z E E H L I S T U E T R S
H C E O I L O L E E I Q O N E H R O R
E T G L T N E R D Z G X H U I T A P F
S X X Q U S G V O N J P O L E O F O Y
T W H N R R Y S A K E U V O D T O L A
E Y P P O K L M M R G T G Y Q K S I A
R K M T I D U Y G S T R S T P O E S S
F B I H Q X N R U H U A E R R O I G C
I D X M B O A W Q I Q Y K U T R Z E R
E E R S C H O O L M A S T E R F E H C
L R E K D C X Q W C M O Y P J O S L Z
D B F F J I V H B W E F G E F O P R M
N O I T A C U D E T N E L L E C X E P
Q M S A Q E V E N I N G P A P E R Q R
```

The Man with the Twisted Lip
Confession Pt. 3 (pages 156–157)

```
S S O M E T I M E L A T E R G T A
J E M P L O Y E R S E C N I F Q E
A C F A V J I G W Y L J E Z J E W
Y A D I L O H C F E M N B M F Q B
P R N D Y I R R D N R B A X W S O
D N G T T A N I Z Q O E Q C I Q U E
N S M H G E S L S M T Y K G T U D R
E T E E N O U C D Y T T E N P E O
S H G D A G Z R Y X A W D I C E M
T I G T E R A Q K O K M D Z G I N E
I W N I T W Z Y D T N Z N G K I L T
W N F T D I S G U I S E D D P B T T
K T V Z C E C A D M S D P B T T I
Y R J H L W C P A E W I E M Y A Y
G O V I E R N C I V W E K R A G L
N F M N S I M A W Y U U Z X C I F
U A M A Y T D E B W Q I P A U X H
```

The Man with the Twisted Lip
Confession Pt. 4 (pages 158–159)

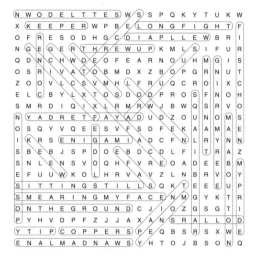

The Man with the Twisted Lip
Confession Pt. 6 (pages 162–163)

The Man with the Twisted Lip
Confession Pt. 5 (pages 160–161)

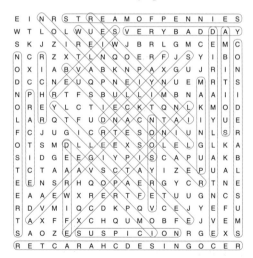

The Man with the Twisted Lip
Confession Pt. 7 (pages 164–165)

The Man with the Twisted Lip Confession Pt. 8 (pages 166–167)

Another Resident of Baker Street (page 168)

In the television show *House*, the title character, Gregory House, was partly inspired by and has many characteristics in common with the fictional detective even though the mysteries he solved were medical instead of criminal. Shore, the show's creator, was a big fan. House, like his predecessor, was irascible, had a companion (James Wilson instead of John Watson), and even lived on Baker Street! The names House, in fact, sounds like "homes," a homonym of the detective's name.

What Went Missing? (pages 169–170)

The chess set. When the client and chess set were found, it turned out the diamond was hidden in one of the pieces.

Duality (page 171)

Many actors have played Holmes, and many have played Watson—but British actor Patrick Macnee was one of the few to play both roles during a long career! He played the character of Watson opposite Roger Moore and Christopher Lee. And to cap it off, in 1984, he played a character on the television show *Magnum P.I.* who had a delusion that he was Sherlock Holmes.

The Red-Headed League Characters (pages 172–173)

The Red-Headed League
Passage 1 (pages 174–175)

```
Z L H R R V U Y T Y Z L R K W
R G N I L Z Z U P J D G P T C
B T W V R F E L U R A S A A R
E R R A Z I B E R O M E C Y T
F E A T U R E L E S S Y O P R
S A U X E H X V E A Y M U F
I Y T O P U I G X I W O M J T
O L E S S M Y S T E R I O U S
S Z M G L G R N Z P C I N A Q
M E E A Y S E M O U X H P X Y
L Z V Z T D M H F I A H L O D
U U M O I T A B R J L L A Z D
M K Z W R C E A X U H I C U Z
Y C D N O P I R P W W U E T C
M O S T D I F F I C U L T C B
```

Passage 3 (pages 178–179)

```
H R E M E M B E R O T H E R W I S E A
F A C T U P O N F A C T Y C P I T T A
M K D G N I R A D E C B E G M T V P W
T Z G P R X F M X D R E M A R K E D A
R A E P N N A Y O V G J G A E U W B L
Z Y X H P B M C T V K I D G L C C B U
U V T P C R T S G N M Y N P I S I F
S E R L I O O U E A T J W T M T E R E
O C A H R Z X P T U L O G L I S G R I
T N O T K J J I O Y D Y Y V S C D Q T
H R O J H O O K S O Q A U Y I E I S
E U D F J N S N K G I B L R R Y L H E
R E I Q P F M A O K S T F N E H W O F
A N A W R E G N A R T S O G W N X Q
Y T R D B R R N E F F O R T N C K K M
W C Y X D N U O R E M O C K X W C E C
U M I S S M A R Y S U T H E R L A N D
H O Q S M Z U B K O P D O U B T I N G
```

Passage 2 (pages 176–177)

```
N E I G H B O U R S X K D
L O P P R E S S E D T C E A
B J P X D O K Y J R L C A L
E U T R U S T T T O H L I
E D S M E E H E K W T N N G
V I E T I O S P E S V Z F I
I N U X N R N W A Q F U G
D E P D D E E E T R U S S S
E P I T E O S D S I D E N O
N A P D K U Q G S E O E D O
T I A I Z U O S C N N V J U
U H T W A V B V T M S L G
A V Y V I H N A Z B E E Y
```

Passage 4 (pages 180–181)

```
N B S I G A H Y E T A S O T F D Q X C
A J B D R A W R O F T S U R H T G O T
M A O Z W D T O K N E E S H M C T
S N O I T A C I D N I V Z G E P R M F
E E V F B E C A L Z I C A B A S L O W
D R B I K O N D P K R V N B A U B J
A R K N Q J U D A J E V I S I T O R D
R S R S J D P Z E R L O E B C F U K M
T L A P H G R D A A N D W N Q A C P F
H I M E L Q Q G S P V R Q F C S Z G P
S F Y C A F E I Y N Y O R F D H P L A
I F R T K O O L D O O G U P L I O S
L E I J O C E C Z L H Y R C O M M C S
R V E N U W U H B L M M Q K X D O E V
B P H Q V W D S P G F S R P G P U D
K C S S X A P P E A R A N C E F S V H
T A V Z T E X L O F L A T T E N E D Q
A D V E R T I S E M E N T C O L U M N
```

The Red-Headed League
Passage 5 (pages 182–183)

```
L T U N T M Z A R E N R O C S
N H X Z N A I R A T E G E V U
E Z O T B I B L U D U T F Q B
W H L B Y Z E A R D E P O T U
S P G P E L K O C D X P O J R
P A E E P Y E M L C Q N C X B
A E N I L E H T G N O L A O A
P B H D O J Y X M I E N O R N
E O A M O R T I M E R S I M K
R Z V S B N H N J R S J E S V
S L O J O T B S X G N E A A T
H O U D M C F A R L A N E S L
O B N C O B U R G B R A N C H
P O E F S M S T A N D I N G R
L E X A C T K N O W L E D G E
```

The Red-Headed League
Newspaper Listing (pages 186–187)

```
M P L A N I M O N Y L E R U P
G T J H F F L X R M I B M T R
W D J A N O N A B E L O K W Y
E L B I G I L E A O F D C E X
A N J S Y A S X C Z D Y O N A
C W X S S W R G V T Z A L T S
B A Y O B R F V A C A N C Y B
Q R O R B E Q U E S T D O O S
Y S A N E B T E V J H M N N E
X A X A O M I V H O A I E E L
E W D C J E J Y T Y I N V Y T
O A A N D M A H J P K D E E I
S H M D W M B O I F Z Y E R N
B Y F L E E T S T R E E T S E
```
```
                              T
                              N
                              U
                              O
                              C
                              C
                              A
                              N
                              O
```

The Red-Headed League
Passage 6 (pages 184–185)

```
W C O N S I D E R A B L E
R M A N U A L L A B O U R
I Q N L O X Z Y J C P G E
T N A O S S I S C Y K B L
I B W N T P A U H M X V I
N A U N Z H P M F O A F M
G F N J K A I K E Y O Y S
F E G I T S V N W E B K A
O E A I H P J L G W R Q H
B Q O S N C J F T E V F T
B N Q U I C K E Y E L S I
O B V I O U S F A C T S W
Q U E S T I O N I N G Z E
```

Stop, Thief! (page 188)

Did you know that the famous detective lost his first case? His first case on film, that is. In 1900, a short silent film called, "Sherlock Holmes Baffled," was created. In the film, an intruder repeatedly comes into frame and steals from the sleuth. As promised in the title, the burglar gets away unscathed. Of course, the film only runs thirty seconds, so perhaps justice would have prevailed if the filmstrip had continued.

What Do You See? (pages 189–190)

Picture 4 is a match.

For His Generation (page 191)

Jeremy Brett played the sleuth in a long-running television series produced by Granada Television in the eighties and nineties. Forty-two of Arthur Conan Doyle's stories were adapted for the series, and the series had a reputation for being faithful to the books. Brett had actually played Watson in 1980, across from Charlton Heston's Holmes.

The Adventure of the Copper Beeches (pages 192–193)

In Cap and Cape (page 194)

Doyle's stories were serialized in a magazine called *The Strand*, and accompanied by illustrations created by Sidney Paget. The idea that Holmes wore a deerstalker cap and an Inverness cape comes not directly from Doyle but from Paget's illustrations. Paget had two brothers, both illustrators; by one account, brother Walter was originally intended to do the first illustrations, but the publishers sent the letter to Sidney instead.

What Do You See? (pages 195–196)

Picture 4 is a match.

What Changed? (pages 197–198)

They flipped the labels on Iodum and Arnica.

An Enduring Trait (page 199)

The detective's signature calabash pipe was popularized by William Gillette, who played Holmes on stage in the late 1800s and early 1900s. Sidney Paget's illustrations showed the sleuth with a straight pipe, but Gillette used a curvy calabash pipe, a detail that lasted in the decades that followed.

The Adventure of the Resident Patient (pages 200–201)

```
B Z S E L P M A X E E E L X K W N
V I P U U E C A L P N O M M O C K
R L S L X N L I N C O H E R E N T
X L R A J U S T I F I E D T Y F B
E U E V K M D L K H K A J O T F I
M S A P N J B E L Z S M E U H P O
S T S P Q U A L L Y C S E R G U G
Y R O A P N V Q F C F P U D I R R
U A N E U J G S F O I X O E L P A
R T I C I T A M A R D N G F S O P
E E N L I T G Q L U N I O O L S H
S A G M M D E C N U O N O R P E E
E N D E A V O R E D P O T C H O R
A S I D B Y R A H C U M Q E U C P
R S J Q N O I T A G I T S E V N I
C N A I R O T S I H D C C T R K B
H P E C U L I A R I T I E S U Y O
```

Celebrating Sherlock (page 202)

The Baker Street stop on the London Underground has tiles that show the silhouette of the most famous (if fictional) resident of that street. Nearby is a museum devoted to the man and his work.

What Went Missing? (pages 203–204)

The pair of scissors went missing.

What Went Missing? (pages 205–206)

One of the couch pillows went missing (the documents were stuffed inside).

Murder and Stolen Gems (page 207)

1	2	3	4	5	6	7	8	9	10	11	12	13
J	A	D	E	C	N	Q	K	V	R	U	B	Y
14	15	16	17	18	19	20	21	22	23	24	25	26
M	Z	T	L	G	X	F	S	O	P	H	I	W

The Cat Burglar (pages 208–209)

Years	Cities	Items	Months
1963	London	sapphires	October
1970	Berlin	gold bars	September
1977	Vancouver	emeralds	July
1984	Paris	cash	June
1991	Antwerp	diamonds	April
1998	Seattle	rubies	May

Marked Bills (pages 210–211)

Dates	Serials	Locations	Denominations
April 1	G-718428	Torbin	$50
April 5	F-667280	Midvale	$100
April 9	B-492841	Uteville	$5
April 13	C-918303	Nettleton	$10
April 17	P-101445	Finsberg	$20

Rare Wines (pages 212–213)

Vintages	Wines	Types	Countries
1954	Weimerund	syrah	Italy
1958	Ania Branco	pinot noir	Spain
1962	Friambliss	pinot gris	Portugal
1966	Ece Suss	chardonnay	Greece
1970	Vendemmia	merlot	France

Stolen Street Signs (pages 214–215)

Dates	Signs	Streets	Streets
July 4th	One Way	Dwight St.	Ralston Ave.
July 11th	Speed Limit	Casper Blvd.	Tarragon Ln.
July 18th	Dead End	Amble Ln.	Quinella St.
July 25th	Yield	Barnacle Rd.	Selby St.
August 1st	Stop	Falstaff St.	Oracle Rd.
August 8th	No Parking	Everett Ave.	Peabody Ln.

A Case of Identity (pages 216–217)

```
B W X Q O O V H L D Y X G D A R L
Z W A M Y H O S M E R A N G E L E
M Q S K G C F Q I C W A H U Z O T
U L B R H G S K Y P L G O D B L O
O Y L I U A W H O R P C L E V J H
Y P U A A O P K E F E L V N G A S
O Z G M H L I H N D I I N E H M A
J E S U O N T V R R P P C L P E R
N B E M G U E I X A Q O S O C P S
U B U H S T A D K S J E O N S W I
S S B Y W F T I A X T F W U N I D
Q I R W F F V E E E X S M C U D I
M A Y A T S H I W I L H D O F I T
M Q O Y W P I O E N M C E T F B A
G A S S F I T T E R S B A L L N
F E N C H U R C H S T R E E T N K
T S H W L V K Q H M F N Z M B K
```

A Case of Identity Passage 2 (pages 220–221)

```
G P I N T R I C A T E M A T T E R M Y
H S I S Y L A N A K C I U Q M I E O M
S E L L I E S R A M M S F B K C C F I
V X L B P M F S G Z B T X I W Y E I B
A E A I D R I O G Z W A A V G N R V P
J O R L D A E N H M J K Q T E G R E I
B N G Y V H B S V G A E T N R V E N V
N J E X M C S P E E W N S K N S D R N
O I F R N R A A Y F N S C U L N E T L I
T A R O M O V Y I C V S I D T Q M M J
A U I F V D D A M L K D V G G Y E G O
R E Z Y M P A X H Y P I K V B F A Y U L A
E S W C L V K E N Q U M X C E I K V
S S V D A W Y L R T G Q T C R P L O I
B J A U Y I V T F S W B B E Y E P D N
O Y S U N I M P O R T A N T S T J Z D
R U C A U S E A N D E F F E C T A P W
```

A Case of Identity Passage 1 (pages 218–219)

```
E I N F I N I T E L Y S T R A N G E R
L X C F D Q N C U N K H Q R N X W C B
B Y R L F K U N A M F O D N I M U O M
A L O I M C M E E Z X X H D I J K N W
T V S T N E V E F O S N I A H C V O
I F E S T I G E N E R A T I O N S L E
F R P W O U L D N O T D A R E P L N L
O I U D Q H E J F M Z H Z Z D O T L F
R M P J T M V D O K N S N N G S G O R
N I O X I N G M M I G Y F A E N I K A
U X S K C L I P D E I X E H Y S N A E
L W E W T D N A H N I D N A H U G L L
U R S T A M C T O D U V T S O O S I L
S E C N E D I C N I O C E G N A R T S
J C K D R E V I E C N O C D L R Z I X
X Q H N G S F O O R E H T E V O M E R
K Y I N I P U G R Z V Q B Y O Z C S T
U P E C N E T S I X E R I L I U S T O
```

A Case of Identity Passage 3 (pages 222–223)

```
V E K Q M H W N L H F I M S K L P
E L A Z C O F F E E C O L O U R R R
G L D N Y E G P Q E B R N V E I T
N V W Q H O R E H T A E F G A E I
I R E O K F R S G T G A I N L K B D
R F A R Z U N C D L V N I A C E T D E
A Y Y T E F M V R G F E J O L P H R
X G H L N E G X R N B X U L V W H
V O R L M N C O E P A K E V D A S I
U I N U O T H T F G D E E F C E A R I
B G G D E R U O L O C E T A L S C K
U W H O Z M Z X H S I Y E R G B B
S H Q O Y X D H A B G L O V E S
I O V R S G N I R R A E D L O G B
P U R P L E P L U S H U W M G Y V
```

A Case of Identity Passage 4
(pages 224–225)

```
E C N A T R O P M I  T  Y  E
I T I S T R U E V V  V  S  C
P C W A X N K O K S  U  R  O
B O M L B C J L H R  O  N  N
L U N K E R Q I J O  T  O  C
Q L D M F T A W E N  C  S  E
U R E A Y T H L Z O  S  S  N
I V R W E W R O N P  U  E  T
C C F D Y Y O P D U  S  R  R
K A U I C R U R E T  A  P  A
E F L O D X E Y D I  G  M  T
Y C L M Q C P V T H  R  I  E
E I Y E V E R Y T H  I  N  G
```

A Case of Identity Passage 5
(pages 226–227)

```
V C O L D B L O O D E D S C O U N D R E L
D M D N S P E T S T F I W S O W T T B B X
S U D F L L C G E M I R C O T E M I R C
I I T Q G W N R R I E A S H O U L D E R S N
U L Q I B Z I V R I A S H O U L D E R S N
O W H J E L L M K T K F K L E M E E E D E
X C O E Z S O H S G S C L P U R G K E E I
N H S W O L L A G C R H O O G R M V T B L
H E U T L A Y A W H Y T L K O D T I C U
E U P O R C G N I T N U H Q N I E S I T Y
A D D O Y X C U R B W T X U D U T E E T
V D P N G H D E U N I T N O C C L Y A E B
D U Q L N C V C F J I F J E O D M T R R
N D A I I C U V E Q I N P W A I L N S X
H I I X B G Z W O F N M S Q L Z V W Y N X
L E S B D M B R O T H E R G J B H W S E G
L L H Z E H F W E R R U N R Z I J P E A
D A M L K P O R A E H U F X P O A G L R Q
O W E H U I E Q M R O T L A Y X T J F H
O Z N F T S H O N Y W I L D C L A T T E R U
R S T N T H S T O P O F H I S S P E E D U
```

The Master Forger (pages 228–229)

Prices	Paintings	Countries	Artists
$1,000,000	Baby Jane	Germany	Greta Frank
$2,000,000	Cold Hills	Canada	Inga Howell
$4,000,000	Day of Night	Portugal	Margot Lane
$8,000,000	Forever Blue	France	Hal Garrison
$16,000,000	Awestruck	Spain	Freda Estes
$32,000,000	Eighteen	Norway	Lyle Kramer

Witness Statements (pages 230–231)

Heights	Witnesses	Weights	Cars
5' 2"	Russell T.	190 lbs	Chevrolet
5' 5"	Sarah M.	145 lbs	Toyota
5' 8"	Yolanda V.	135 lbs	Honda
5' 11"	Angela S.	225 lbs	Mazda
6' 2"	Gerald F.	160 lbs	Nissan

The Adventure of the Copper Beeches Letter Pt. 1 (pages 232–233)

```
E L E C T R I C B L U E P R D
J G N I S A H C R U P A B A E
E N A T T R A C T E D N G L S
W I U S D K T C N B S X I U C
D G G N I T C A X E C I U C R
G N I L L I W D I K Y O Y I I
L O E B Q E E K N G C U L T P
N L N H W C L C D H A S D R T
W E J C I E H H O V Z L N A I
N B E S N E P M O C E R I P O
G N I N R O M U R N D C K C N
X O P H N E C S S E R D D A E
N M I N C O N V E N I E N C E
R E C O N S I D E R E D W Q H
P H I L A D E L P H I A Z D Y
```

The Adventure of the Copper Beeches Letter Pt. 2 (pages 234–235)

```
H X M Y X Y P E S O L X V E E H Z
A J R J W L A M M I Y L V C G A S
A I K I J E L S Y Z T T N N N N S
R E F J I U W T V U R T I E O L O
E E S N B V F K U X V A I S D E G L
T N I E R H M A B X R F Q N D D X
S E A W E T F E A A I S D E G S L
E P M Y T I P B M D M S N V Z U
H M E Y N U E N J N R O N E F L
C O R U I F R C M S E B J O R E
A E W T R Z J N B X H L N I Y S
I E W T R T Z J N B X H L N I Y S
W R X X O K H O N Z N O E I D L E
J R A H H E C B E A L X I C T I I
R E L T S A C U R O R H P E J G T
I N C R E A S E D S A L A R Y H U
A M U S I N G Y O U R S E L F T D
```

Adventure of the Copper Beeches Passage 1 (pages 236–237)

```
O Y G T C E J B U S L A I C E P S G S
L M N X S C A T T E R E D H O U S E S
Z R I G H E Q E D S Y T B S D Q E S B
B S H P P X Y G J R F E V F E Z U N X
H I T F N P O N K U G N I L I M S E D
W R Y Z R E C I P C H R M T Z E I V F
N J R Z W R O L K G W I P D C S A A A
D E E N O I M E G F S M R N L Y B E C
N T V P N E M E E O W E E M M V C H O
I A E S K N I F L B X R S D T E Q D U
S N I U C T A O U E W S V R Y N O N T
F C L M O E T B B F J B E X T I Q O R
O O Q P Y I E Q E J X B D U M M B G Y
D S U U D R W R W Z A A P J N A F Y
R S Z N D S D A E T S E M O H C U Q S
O A I I D Q R D N S B H O R R I F Y I
C B C T C E R T A I N H O R R O R N D
E P L Y G T D G K W Z M T Q X P P O E
R L O W E S T A N D V I L E S T L Y T
```

Describing Sherlock Holmes (page 238)

"It is not easy to express the inexpressible," he answered with a laugh. "Holmes is a little too scientific for my tastes—it approaches to cold-bloodedness. I could imagine his giving a friend a little pinch of the latest vegetable alkaloid, not out of malevolence, you understand, but simply out of a spirit of inquiry in order to have an accurate idea of the effects. To do him justice, I think that he would take it himself with the same readiness. He appears to have a passion for definite and exact knowledge."

BONUS ANSWER: The character of Stamford, in "A Study in Scarlet"

What Changed? (pages 239–240)

The frying pan flipped.

What Went Missing? (pages 241–242)

The canister of film had been stolen.

Words of a Genius (page 243)

"But it is a question of getting details. Give me your details, and from an armchair I will return you an excellent expert opinion. But to run here and run there, to cross-question railway guards, and lie on my face with a lens to my eye—it is not my metier. No, you are the one man who can clear the matter up. If you have a fancy to see your name in the next honours list—"

BONUS ANSWER: The speaker is Mycroft Holmes in "The Adventure of the Bruce-Partington Plans"

Bank Robberies (pages 244–245)

Dates	Banks	Towns	Amounts
June 3	First Trust	Longwood	$1,000
June 5	Moneycorp	Yountville	$1,600
June 7	Wellspring	Tahoe	$4,800
June 9	Bell Largo	Grumley	$2,500
June 11	Apex	Cold Spring	$10,200

The Adventure of the Greek Interpreter (pages 246–247)

The Reigate Puzzle (pages 250–251)

The Adventure of the Norwood Builder (pages 248–249)

Fingerprint Match (page 252)

The matching pairs are: A and K; B and I; C and L; D and J; E and H; F and N; G and P; M and O

What Went Missing? (pages 253–254)

The row of four serving spoons went missing.

What Do You See? (pages 255–256)

Picture 3 is a match.

What Went Missing? (pages 257–258)

The nail polish went missing.

What Went Missing?
(pages 259–260)

The keys went missing.

Fingerprint Match (page 261)

The matching pairs are: A and G; B and H; C and E; D and F

The Bascombe Valley Mystery
(pages 262–263)

The Bascombe Valley Mystery
Passage 1 (pages 264–265)

The Bascombe Valley Mystery
Passage 2 (pages 266–267)

The Bascombe Valley Mystery Passage 3 (pages 268–269)

```
H R P A H P C L S U I X Y D J M N
A D E L O S N O C E C I N L S J F
N D E H I T K Z V U F R H B Y C I
G V S R Q E F I W D I A M R A B B
E L L Q E X L F L Y U Y T E D C E
D B I T O F N E W S O L K H E A T
M H I E O T F U T C X R B H E R R
C S E M G K R U U E S E K R R R E
C A P A P E R S S U Y T Q G H C E
A V H F O O M B R I S T O L T G U
R U I T R O R N I K C U R T T Q B
T E L B U O R T S U O I R E S L I
H D N A B S U H A O G L J Y A O L
Y P J U L I I G Y N W Z J D L V Y
U B E R M U D A D O C K Y A R D D
E X R W X C P O J C B E Q T E E S
Y K N U T N I O P T A H T K R A M
```

The Con Artist (pages 270–271)

Months	Names	Towns	Careers
March	Abe Avery	Valero	accountant
April	Fred Flores	Opalville	doctor
May	Matt Mintz	Nanaimo	reporter
June	Sean Starr	Beaverton	bank mgr.
July	Pat Perry	Trippany	dentist
August	Lou Lemon	Hoople	lawyer

The Adventure of the Speckled Band (pages 272–273)

```
G R I M E S B Y R O Y L O T T
R S T O K E M O R A N D B S V
R O H E L E N S T O N E R P R
G B T F A R I N T O S H E E E
K F A A O K U K J B M A H C D
N Q A B L U K S P Q I T F K D
I L T G O I C Q L R A E N L A
A I T I X O T H O F I F L E P
R A U X H I N N P J W G S D M
M H C Y Y A O E E D I N Q B A
I P L Y E H T G V A C H A W
T A U R S M E A K T W I N S
A S C Z R K M R E X W A T D L
G E T G U A G K A H Z W Y F N
E W B E S N B K E F C T F H V
```

The Adventure of the Speckled Band Story Pt. 1 (pages 274–275)

```
A M O N G T H E R I C H E S T M I H E
W A S T E F U L D I S P O S I T I O N
Y W V B B F U C H Q A U R K C N B Z R
C O Q T S M E T L K O G E E N M P T D
N J Z H E J M W E V J N J Z L O C L U
D H I R D P R A W U E B B T B O H Q
G K E E I P I M X C M O E R Y H M C G
E N A T H H K S F D R E R V R D P A A
R C V L S S Y B S D C E Q S U E L W G
N B Y P K Z L B E O A Y S A T H E H I
P U M M R P M R M B L U W G N S T K W
W A O A E H S L T E H U U Z E U E C G
H Q R C B Z O O Q Z Y W T G C R D S
Q E T B R N J V G W H K F D E T C E U E
X T G J L O L D S H Z Q D S T B X E
P E A N I U R Y L I M A F V A P F B U
Y Y G F B N P P T I Q Q K T L E C I I
D Q E S R I E H E V I S S E C C U S A
T W O H U N D R E D Y E A R O L D T P
```

The Adventure of the Speckled Band Story Pt. 2 (pages 276–277)

```
X W V J C A P I T A L S E N T E N C E
V O T P A D A I I G T P O E A L M M Y
J S M E E V D E N R U T E R B N O E D
H Q V X V D U B H U X U E U E R D E
L G O I Y M U E O E M R C C I N C A
L A S T S Q U I R E Q I B Y L K S C A
H G L A S T E P F A T H E R E A E A R
R C M L R G X I X C B C T P R C C L T
E O M E L R G P A K F W X M Q U Y D
A M E B N O P E E D N Z M X D D I G R
B E Y B E E F I T O F A N G E R U R E
L P Z R G R E X I S T E N C E E P
D R K J I H A T Q M V Z I W L E S
R A F O R C E O F C H A R A C T E R A
Y L K C W A R I S T O C R A T I C N H
D I S A P P O I N T E D O N B R L U L
H O R R I B L E L I F E V C O L M W D
P R O F E S S I O N A L H W C W O Q R
```

The Adventure of the Speckled Band Story Pt. 3 (pages 278–279)

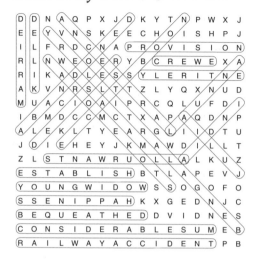

```
D D N A Q P X J D K Y T N P W X J
E E Y V N S K E E C H O I S H P J
I L F R D C N A P R O V I S I O N
R L N W E O E R Y B C R E W E X A
R I K A D L E S S Y L E R I T N E
A K V N R S L T T Z L Y Q X N U D
M U A C I O A I P R C Q L U F D I
I B M D C C M C T X A P A Q D N P
A L E K L T Y E A R G L I I D T U
J D I E H E Y J K M A W D I L L T
Z L S T N A W R U O L L A L K U Z
E S T A B L I S H B T L A P E V J
Y O U N G W I D O W S S O G O F O
S S E N I P P A H K X G E D N J C
B E Q U E A T H E D D V I D N E S
C O N S I D E R A B L E S U M E B
R A I L W A Y A C C I D E N T P B
```

The Adventure of the Speckled Band Story Pt. 5 (pages 282–283)

```
W J B M N G A Y W E A O P H A R R O W
A L F A O W O R K O F T H E H O U S E
L N Y J G E S M O C Q R M A I D E N N
G N O R E W I S H T O S P E A K R K I
Y N L R E M Q O R X D M W A X D V P G
Z O A O A N O I T I S O P D N A E G A
L I N F T Q J Y U X A W T A F Q U M M
O N T O M P D E P R I V E D A N L B Y J
N C I A L T E S H O R T V I S I T S V
G E S R E T S I S R O O P N F W O H R
T J A I A E W L I T L D A X E V V N E
I B C N S Y Z B Z I V H N F O T R Z T
M O C E U Q L H O E L H A A R K I N Y
C N B T E S A M T S I R H C V U E W
Q T K V N I L T T H G I N T R O F O L
C Z E N L I T T L E L I K E L Y M N S
U N G Y T R I H T T W E S T P H A I L
T W O Y E A R S A G O N I L S J A J I
```

The Adventure of the Speckled Band Story Pt. 4 (pages 280–281)

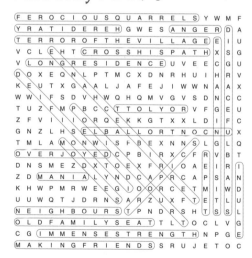

```
F E R O C I O U S Q U A R R E L S Y W M F
Y R A T I D E R E H G W E S A N G E R D A
T E R R O R O F T H E V I L L A G E E I U
V C L E H T C R O S S H I S P A T H X S G
V L O N G R E S I D E N C E U V E E C G U
D O X E Q N L P T M C X D N R H U I H R V
K E U T X G A A L J A F E J I W W N A A C
W W I F S D V H W Q H Q M V G V S D N C C
T U Z F M P B C C T T O L Y O R V F G E U
Z F V I I O R Q E K K G T X X L D I F C L
G N Z L H S E L B A L L O R T N O C N U X
T M L A M O N W I S F B E X N N S L G L Q
O V E R J O Y E D C P B I R X C F R V B T
D N S M E Z D X T O E X F R I O A E I R I
Z D M A N I A L Y N D C A P R C A P S N D
K H W P M R W E E G I O O R C E T M I W U
U U W Q T J D R N S A R Z U X F T E T L S
N E I G H B O U R S T P N D R S H T S S
O L D F A M I L Y S E A T T L T O C L V G
C G I M M E N S E S T R E N G T H N P G E
M A K I N G F R I E N D S S R U J E T O C
```

The Adventure of the Speckled Band Death Pt. 1 (pages 284–285)

```
T C L O S E L Y A L L I E D R F I
H S N V Q B N H Q C K G J S A R A
G L H I V A G U E F E E L I N G K
I U T R L E V B C U W D T B H W Y
N O P O A R N B U R S T F O R T H
D S Z D T W U U E L T B U S S N Q
L I W R I E J V B T E U R B G T O C
I W T E R M K J I S R W Z N H N T G
W T C R F Q Y N X V O I Z S E S G
M D O O O R Z D H B H F H A M L I
U N L C S S J C Z S E A S S O E N I
W I L D S C R E A M W A C I M E G
J B E W A V N L C L Q D T Y M P N A
N S C F M X P B H I U V R I S M A L
D E T E D S T G A K K P X Y N R L C
U T E R R I F I E D W O M A N G C
L O W W H I S T L E M G P E A Z D
```

The Adventure of the Speckled Band Death Pt. 2 (pages 286–287)

```
N S E G N I H Q X S C Y N K I Z W N D
I S A U A R R Y L R Q A K H Q D B E E
A X P A S S A G E O V W I D F E W K S
P Z A I X S Q N W R M E H G F H N C L
E D L X L L I W R R F V K N Y C Y I U
L L I M B S E Y I E I I L Q N Q R V U
B D K P Z K R X T H G W L C A Q T N O
I F P U J W D S H M Q O R D H L N S O
R W P G D I G Y E U L E J O U B S R C
R X X W K C Z R D S T I C C Q W G O Y
E N P M A L R O D I R R O C A R S R L
T D M J U B O E L T U B P Y O T F R L
I R X Y N D V I O J Q A I P G C M O U
N A A Y L L I B W R A N I G N B H H H
S K R I O R B N E P G N S N I Z S N D
T N Y V C X L G P P G H K O N F K S A
F U E V K S E E N K H K S P E G M A E
R R Q A E C A E A Q U S O A P Z B A R
F D E J D R Y H Z B P G V P O J K B D
```

The Adventure of the Engineer's Thumb (pages 290–291)

```
F S U O R E D R U M U L T Z L
R E E N I G N E K C P A I X K
B M U H T W X Y M I U C E B R
E K F S Y C P F A L P I F N A
K M X U Q A G O D U A R R O T
G G A G L A B R P A L E E S S
E S R O H L B D B R E T T U R
W S P T W E E D R D D S N G E
N P Z T C B S R Q Y L Y U R D
C H B H Z U R E S H N H O E N
T V E F Y E T L V E U X C F A
Y R P I V S A R F R A H Z C S
V I C T O R H A T H E R L E Y
V W Z D V X J O A O C N T D L
R E V A E L C T D W R Z T H P
```

The Adventure of the Speckled Band Death Pt. 3 (pages 288–289)

```
Y B N M W A X N D V D Y D M A M E M D S K
A Z G Y R U G R E O C H U V B X F I S V N
R T K V X E O Q C V C R R H X U A P U A A S
B S S G B R T T D R E A D F U L E N D S S
V P B U K N O S E H P R S E A P D Y D C Y
C C O A O R C C I M A P F C T I E V E M L
N R X U S I O U C S E S I O A G F R N I O
E E X R R G O C D C D D T S R N K G L S O
V C O U N E R S K J E X E E E W G R F Y F I
R O S I C I D L N M A V V O N I E N S I S
M V S U O X E B U O A T G O V I X T H N A
M E N Q J D E X R H C G H Z L D N W R G R
D R B E B S U G N A N N E R X E E G I E F
S E G A L Z E I A I N M U K O W B L E R F
T D N R A E A G S L C D U I Y A Y N N K N
A D A X V F H S D M L U Y M N P T S E B P
B I K D J D E A B Q J I F G W Z M D M E
B W P T N R N O I S L U V N O C H S E R F
E I U R D C A L L I N G L O U D L Y B K T
D Q F O S D R O W R E H D E K O H C R R Q
J J B A P I A U K D W G U B O P C K L X B
```

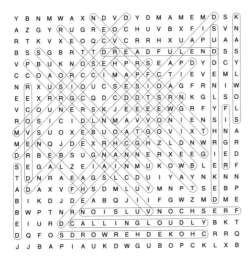

The Adventure of the Engineer's Thumb Passage 1 (pages 292–293)

```
X S C T Y X A P O F G N C J X Y V O Q
L A A P E Z U P H W Y O B I V A G U E
Q H X C B T U J F O W F D H V X H L Q
H Q I Y I C W H A V E T O T E L L U W
D T X K R T X Q I E B O Z J P W B O O
F L C R S A N P L G U E T V A S I K U
L A J G P S N K R R F R L Y P O B Y N
B M S U R P R I S E D Y O I T Y W V D
X L P V J I Q E D G V F D L E V N H O
T N B Y I E L Q T R P A I N E V F J F
H V R P C V U K Z R O W B C L U E S M
T W Q I E M E O D N A Y X U C D D I
M W L S S E I O Q K R C R Q I Y V C N
B O W T S T F W J Q H I R T Z O C Z E
P H I C K R Y A L Q T O S G X F Z M N
T O R Q D O K F O L U U R Q K E O K K
N J Y O H M R H Y X J H B N V K D Y D
C O N V I N C I N G E V I D E N C E S
L R X H T N E M E T A T S T E C Y U O
```

The Adventure of the Engineer's Thumb Passage 2 (pages 294–295)

The Adventure of the Engineer's Thumb Passage 3 (pages 296–297)

Telephone Records (pages 298–299)

Times	People	Numbers	Lengths
1:52am	Kerry	239-4827	22 seconds
1:57am	Charlie	447-6995	3 minutes
2:02am	Vicky	731-9262	48 seconds
2:07am	Mitchell	592-0021	35 seconds
2:12am	Sarah	368-7841	1.5 minutes

The Adventure of the Noble Bachelor (pages 300–301)

The Adventure of the Noble Bachelor Letter (pages 302–303)

The Adventure of the Noble Bachelor Article Pt. 1
(pages 304–305)

The Adventure of the Noble Bachelor Article Pt. 3
(pages 308–308)

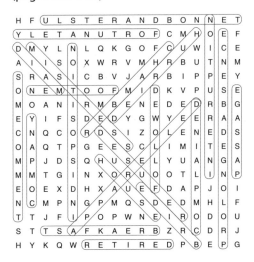

The Adventure of the Noble Bachelor Article Pt. 2
(pages 306–307)

The Adventure of the Noble Bachelor Article Pt. 4
(pages 310–311)

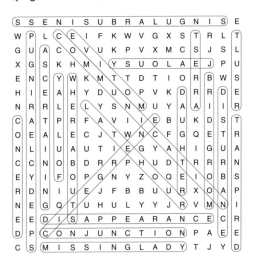

Smuggled Electronics
(pages 312–313)

Departures	Flights	Gates	Items
8:03am	108	11	watches
8:10am	233	18	televisions
8:17am	356	3	tablets
8:24am	510	6	cell phones
8:31am	92	7	laptops

The Adventure of Black Peter
(pages 314–315)

Crack the Password (page 316)
The missing letter is O.

noise, primrose, loaner, mosaic

Crack the Password (page 317)
The missing letter is L.

amoral, central, flamingo, musical

The Adventure of the Beryl Coronet Letter (pages 318–319)

The Adventure of the Beryl Coronet Passage 1 (pages 320–321)

Grave Robberies (pages 322–323)

Dates	Cemeteries	Graves	Towns
March 12th	Box Grove	Brad Beaudry	Verona
March 20th	Apple Pine	Ruben Yates	Upperdale
March 28th	Green Lawn	Pat Fowler	Shell City
April 5th	Calvary Cape	Holden Bray	Wilmette
April 13th	Dinby Dale	Ed Lowder	Trenton

The Five Orange Pips
(pages 324–325)

The Five Orange Pips Tragedy
Pt. 2 (pages 328–329)

The Five Orange Pips Tragedy
Pt. 1 (pages 326–327)

The Five Orange Pips Passage 1
(pages 330–331)

The Five Orange Pips Passage 2
(pages 332–333)

Famous First Lines (page 334)

1. E; 2. C; 3. D; 4. A. 5. B

Fill in the Empty House (page 335)

1. B; 2. A; 3. A; 4. C; 5. B

The Adventure of the Golden Pince-Nez (pages 336–337)

International Fugitives (pages 338–339)

Dates	Criminals	Crimes	Countries
October 3	Grendle	robbery	Peru
October 4	Dornmer	forgery	Moldova
October 5	Filcher	tax evasion	France
October 6	Blackforth	arson	Uganda
October 7	Calumnet	blackmail	Sweden

Charles Augustus Milverton
(pages 340–341)

Solve a Crime (page 342)

Answers may vary. CRIME, grime, gripe, grips, grins, gains, pains, pairs, hairs, hairy, harry, carry, curry, curvy, curve, carve, calve, salve, SOLVE

Murder Mysteries (page 343)

Answers may vary. MURDERS, mudders, madders, ladders, larders, warders, wanders, ganders, genders, renders, readers, headers, heaters, beaters, betters, batters, matters, masters, mastery, MYSTERY

The Murderous Gem Thief
(page 344)

The count is: 1 diamond, 2 pearls, 3 rubies, 4 sapphires, and 5 pieces of jade.

Murder Method: Shot by Guns
(page 345)

Answers may vary. SHOT, shop, stop, step, stem, seem, sees, sets, gets, guts, GUNS